D0977310

CRUSHING IT!

Also by Gary Vaynerchuk

#AskGaryVee: One Entrepreneur's Take on Leadership, Social Media, and Self-Awareness

Jab, Jab, Jab, Right Hook: How to Tell Your Story in a Noisy Social World

The Thank You Economy

Crush It! Why NOW Is the Time to Cash In on Your Passion

GARY VAYNERCHUK

CRUSHING IT!

HOW GREAT ENTREPRENEURS BUILD THEIR BUSINESS AND INFLUENCE— AND HOW YOU CAN, TOO

HARPER
BUSINESS

An Imprint of HarperCollinsPublishers

CRUSHING IT! Copyright © 2018 by Gary Vaynerchuk. All rights reserved. Printed in the United States of America. No part of this book may be used or reproduced in any manner whatsoever without written permission except in the case of brief quotations embodied in critical articles and reviews. For information, address Harper-Collins Publishers, 195 Broadway, New York, NY 10007.

HarperCollins books may be purchased for educational, business, or sales promotional use. For information, please e-mail the Special Markets Department at SPsales@harpercollins.com.

FIRST EDITION

Designed by William Ruoto

Library of Congress Cataloging-in-Publication Data has been applied for.

ISBN 978-0-06-267467-8

18 19 20 21 22   LSC   10 9 8 7 6 5 4 3 2 1

AUTHOR NOTE

All e-mail excerpts and interviews have been edited for length, content, and clarity.

THIS IS DEDICATED TO ALL
THE PEOPLE WHO ARE
VISIONARY ENOUGH TO
RECOGNIZE THE ENORMOUS
OPPORTUNITIES WE'VE BEEN
GIVEN IN THIS NEW DIGITAL
AGE, AND WHO ARE BRAVE
ENOUGH TO DEMAND AND
SEEK OUT HAPPINESS NOT
ONLY IN THEIR LIFE BUT ALSO
IN THEIR WORK.

CONTENTS

Introduction   1

PART I: GET PUMPED

1 The Path Is All Yours   13
2 What (Still) Matters   29
3 The Eighth Essential—Content   77
4 What's Stopping You?   97
5 The Only Thing You Need to Give Yourself to Crush It   120

PART II: CREATE YOUR PILLAR

6 First, Do This   135
7 Get Discovered   139
8 Musical.ly   143
9 Snapchat   157

10 Twitter   177

11 YouTube   191

12 Facebook   209

13 Instagram   223

14 Podcasts   235

15 Voice-First   245

Conclusion   261

Acknowledgments   265

Notes   267

CRUSHING IT!

INTRODUCTION

My eight-year old daughter, Misha, wants to be a YouTuber when she grows up. That probably comes as no surprise—many young kids find out what their parents do and decide that's their ambition, too (in addition to becoming a firefighter and zoo keeper). My daughter sees me using online platforms to talk to people and build businesses, and she knows how much I love it. Of course she thinks she wants to do what I do.

What might be more surprising is that if you ask other school-age children what they want to be when they grow up, many will reply that they, too, want to be YouTubers.

Personal branding may not be an elementary school Career Day staple yet, but kids today know that making videos on YouTube, posting on Instagram, tweeting 280 characters, and snapping on Snapchat is a valid career path and that for some it can even bring fame and fortune. They dream of creating a popular online presence the way kids used to dream of becoming Hollywood stars. Unfortunately, unless they're entrepreneurs themselves or deeply in the know, most parents will respond to this career aspiration with, "Huh?" or worse, narrow-minded cynicism: "That's not a real job." Even the few who smile uncomprehendingly and offer a mild, "Great, honey! Go for it!" will likely secretly shake their heads at the sweet naïveté of youth.

It's so frustrating to me.

Obviously the first answers suck any way you look at them, but all of these responses reveal a total lack of understanding about what kind of world we live in. It's the kind where an eleven-year-old kid and his dad can become millionaires by creating a YouTube channel where they share online videos of themselves cutting things in half.

I knew this was the way things were going to go. For someone like me with a tendency to make over-the-top pronouncements, it's ironic that one of the most prescient things I've ever uttered may also have been the biggest understatement of my life:

My story is about to become a lot less unusual.

I first made it when Misha was just a newborn, in the introduction to my first business book, *Crush It!* I was recounting how I had used the Internet to develop a personal brand and grow my $4 million family business, Shopper's Discount Liquors, into a $60 million business. My strategy was simple and outrageous for the time: I spoke directly to potential customers through a bare-bones video blog and developed relationships with them on Twitter and Facebook, inviting a direct one-on-one engagement that had previously existed only between merchants and customers in the tight-knit small communities and neighborhoods of the last century. By the time I wrote the book in 2009, I had branched out from my first passion—wine and sales—to my all-encompassing one—building businesses. I was traveling the world spreading the word to anyone who would listen that the platforms most companies and business leaders were still labeling as pointless time wasters—Facebook, Twitter, and YouTube—were actually the future of all business. It seems impossible now, but the digital revolution was so young I actually had to define the platforms. Back then, I had to devote considerable time to explaining that Facebook was this online site where you could share articles and photographs and your feelings and thoughts, and Twitter was something like it except always public and limited to, at the time, 140 characters. Personal branding? No one knew what the hell I was talking about. It's hard to believe it now, but not even a decade ago, the idea that more than a select few people could realistically build a business by using social media was considered far-fetched.

I now run a massive digital media company with offices in New York, Los Angeles, Chattanooga, and London. I'm still engaging people on Twitter, Facebook, Instagram, Snapchat, and any other platform that catches people's attention. I'm still invited to speak all over the world, but I also reach millions of people through my business Q&A YouTube show, #AskGaryVee; my daily video documentary, DailyVee; my role on *Planet of the Apps*—an Apple reality-TV show about app development—and books like the one you're holding in your hand. I'm working more than ever. I'm having more of an impact than ever. I'm happier than ever.

And I am anything but unusual.

Today there are millions of people just like me who have used the Internet to build personal brands, thriving businesses, and a life on their own terms. Those who are truly crushing it have grasped the brass ring of grown-up-hood—building a lucrative business around something they love that enables them to do what they want every day. But while in 2009 that "something" might have been homemade preserves or custom tree houses, today it could also include being a mom, being stylish, or having an unorthodox world view. In other words, you can use your personal brand—who you are—to market your business, or your personal brand can actually *be* the business. Socialites, celebrity progeny, and reality-TV stars have been doing it for years. Now it's everyone else's turn to learn how to get paid to do something they were going to do for free anyway.

A lot has changed since I wrote *Crush It!*, but surprisingly, a lot hasn't. Anyone who follows me regularly knows she can fast-forward through the first ten minutes of my keynote speeches, because I'm just going to repeat the facts of my life and my opinion of the world in pretty much the exact same way that I have been for almost a decade. Once those ten minutes are up, though, you never know. And that's what I'm going to share in this book—the part of the keynote that changes every six to nine months because that's how frequently the platforms evolve. I want you to learn the most up-to-date information on how to best leverage Internet platforms to create a powerful, lasting personal brand.

The biggest difference between my first book and the one you're reading now is this: mine isn't the only voice in this one. I want to introduce you to other entrepreneurs who have met with unbelievable success by following *Crush It!* principles to build their personal brands. Some are internationally well known, some are still climbing their way up. All of them are absolutely loving life. Though each is unique, I suspect you'll be relieved and thrilled to see that they are not that different from you. How can I say that when I don't know you? Because the secret to their success (and mine) had nothing to do with where they came from, whom they knew, where they went to school, or what field they were in. Rather, it had everything to do with their appreciation for the platforms at their disposal and their willingness to do whatever it took to make these social-media tools work to their utmost potential. And that, my friends, is something I can teach you to do, too.

What worked for me won't work for you, however, and vice versa. That's why self-awareness is so vital—you have to be true to yourself at all times. What I can offer you is a set of universal principles. We'll dissect every current major platform so that all of you, from plumbers (your pillar should be Facebook; see page 209) to park rangers (yours is YouTube; see page 191), will know exactly which platform to use as your pillar content, and how to use the other platforms to amplify your personal brands. We'll dissect the social platforms that dominate the business world today. I talked about some of these in *Crush It!*, but they have evolved, and there are now even better ways to navigate them. I'll offer theoretical and tactical advice on how to become the biggest thing on old standbys like Twitter, Facebook, YouTube, and Instagram; younger upstarts like Musical.ly; audiocentric platforms like Spotify, SoundCloud, and iTunes; and newcomer Alexa Skills. Those who have been at this for a while will find useful the little-known nuances, innovative tips, and clever tweaks that have been proven to enhance more common tried-and-true strategies.

If you've been watching me closely for years and you think you know it all, please reconsider. I talk to thousands of people every year, and I hear the same questions over and over again. If so many still haven't perfected their game, there's a good chance you haven't either. Today could be the day that you finally "get" that little nugget of info that's going to help you pulverize whatever has been holding you back. Several of the people interviewed for this book said they read *Crush It!* multiple times. Entrepreneur and podcaster John Lee Dumas revisits it yearly. It's only 142 pages long, not so dense that he couldn't figure out the gist in an hour or so, and yet Dumas admits that he listened to the audiobook three times before he finally understood what I meant about personal branding. That eureka moment led him to found Entrepreneurs on Fire, his daily podcast interviewing the country's most inspiring and innovative entrepreneurs. Today his show is one of the top-ranked business podcasts on iTunes, grossing around $200,000 per month. I know this because he posts his monthly financials on his site and shares the details about his expenditures in his podcast so other entrepreneurs can learn from his smart moves and avoid his mistakes. That's just one example of the kind of surprise and delight the entrepreneurs in this book regularly conjure up to distinguish their personal brands from those of the competition and earn hordes of adoring, loyal fans.

As always, I'm going to be real with you: even if you absorb every lesson and follow every piece of advice in these pages, most of you reading this book will not become millionaires. *Do not stop reading!* None of the people interviewed for this book knew they'd become rich; they became rich because they were incredibly, ridiculously good at what they do and worked so goddamn hard, no one else could keep up. Most started out with modest ambitions of earning enough to enjoy the good things in life, finding stability, supporting themselves and their families, and living on their own terms. Achieve that kind of wealth, and you won't need riches. And who knows, maybe in the process of getting there you, like John Lee Dumas and his cohorts, will discover that you do have the talent and marketing savvy to become a millionaire. There's only one way to find out. Either way, you win. It takes pressure and fire to turn a lump of unremarkable metal into a finely crafted work of art. This book is filled with inspiration and advice from others who have walked through those flames; let them guide you so you can see what you're capable of becoming.

Consider the experience of Louie Blaka (IG: @louieblaka), who explained in an e-mail how he went from art teacher to thriving artist by trusting his instincts and putting his passions to work.

I'm a high school art teacher but a fine artist at heart. Three years ago I decided to give my art career a shot outside of my seven-to-three teaching job. My artwork took off but not as well as I had hoped. I didn't give up, but I did become a bit discouraged. I listened to *Crush It!* two years ago, and it helped me think bigger than just selling paintings. I saw a trend of wine and paint classes taking over the country. I asked myself why I wasn't hosting these classes if I had an actual teaching degree along with the experience of a professional artist (*Duh!*). So I took your advice of marketing through social and held a *free* wine and paint class for my alma mater, Montclair State. I posted a picture of the event on my Instagram, and I started to get inquiries for booking classes. I started with a class of ten people, with maybe one class every two or three months, and I've grown to at least three classes a month with my next class scheduled to host *one hundred people*. I've spent *zero* dollars on marketing, with everything going through IG and word of mouth. I've been able to market my paintings (as an artist) through my wine and paint class customers. I've taken all the unused materials or "waste" from my classes and used them for my personal artwork.

I've been able to grow my personal career as an artist from selling a painting for $200 to having a painting auction for $1,300 at NYC's Coffee Festival this past September. I started my wine and paint business with a free event with about ten people at a college campus, and I'm now hoping to reach $30,000 in sales next year (I know it isn't much, but for a full-time teacher and artist it's *huge*).

The explosion of YouTube and Instagram, the emergence of podcasts, the ubiquity of platforms like Facebook and Twitter—all have led us to the tipping point I predicted nine years ago. You already have the tools to build the kind of powerful personal brand that can change your future. If you've been at this for a while and haven't gotten where you want to go, this book will explain why. If you're a D-lister with your eyes on the A-list, I can help you climb that ladder (and I empathize—I was on the Z-list for years and know what the view is like from down there). If you've been making excuses, you'll be exposed, at which point you can decide to stop dicking around and achieve what you set out to achieve—or admit that your version of crushing it looks a little different than you originally thought it did.

See, this book is for two audiences. The first is people who know to the depths of their souls that they are born to build something great. Natural-born entrepreneurs should find all the information they need to improve their current efforts or start making plans of their own. The second audience is everyone else who wants to work. Not just the young, not just the tech-oriented. Not just professionals in established careers or those looking to renew themselves because they've outgrown their industry or, worse, their industry is shrinking. It's in everyone's best interest to build a personal brand, even if they have little interest in becoming rich or famous. You're not computer savvy? Get the computer or tech skills you need to do this. It is not hard, and many of the people we talked to for this book had as little experience with computers as you do. In case you haven't noticed, no job is particularly stable anymore. Imagine the security you would feel if you had something going on the side that you could blow up big if you unexpectedly had nothing but time (meet Pat Flynn on page 122). Desperation can be a great motivator, but it's a lot less stressful if you plan ahead so that you never know the feeling.

If you're earning what you need to live the life you want *and* loving every day of it, you're crushing it. That's all I want for you. I think of the friends I grew up with who loved video games but whose parents forced them to stop playing because the games were new and scary and distracted them from their studies. Those kids may have grown up to make a decent enough living, but by doing something they tolerate or even hate. If only their parents could have seen how the world would evolve. Maybe the child who became a lawyer to please his or her parents could be earning the same amount now as an eSports (competitive gaming) promoter—or earning millions as a professional e-gamer. Either way, that lawyer would be infinitely happier.

Parents are trying to get their children off Pokémon Go when augmented-reality gaming is going to be huge for generations. They think their daughters should make less slime and do more algebra. Slime may be a fad; slime could also become the conduit through which a girl learns the dynamic of supply and demand on Instagram and builds a million-dollar personal brand and company. The crazy thing is that *she wouldn't be the first*. Karina Garcia did it. She used to be a waitress; now she's a successful YouTube star famous for making, you guessed it, slime. How successful? With six-figure earnings every month, she was able to retire her parents. In August 2017 she took a seven-week, fourteen-city tour to meet her fans. People paid $40.00 to $99.99 for VIP passes. Stories like that are no longer uncommon, and they illustrate why we need to give our children as much freedom as possible to gravitate toward what they love doing. Because in their world, nothing will be off-limits when it comes to how you can make a good living and build a stellar career. When I was a kid making straight Ds and I got caught reading baseball card catalogs in class so I'd know how much to charge for trades, everyone said, "You're going to be a loser." Today they'd say, "You're going to be the next Zuckerberg." When it comes to professional opportunities, this is the best time to be alive in the history of humankind. I don't want anyone to waste it.

If you take away anything valuable or helpful from this book, I hope you will give a copy to someone you care about who is not happy in his or her current job or career. If you are a parent, please give it to your children as they start to imagine what and who they want to be. I say this not because I want to sell more books. Get it from the library; I don't care. I say this because I want everyone to know that these opportunities exist, so that if someone is struggling or miserable or scared, they can do something to change that. If you care about the people in your life, you want them to be happy doing something they love. Life is short; its brevity and unpredictability is the one thing that scares me. It is also long; a fifty-year-old could still look forward to another forty or even fifty productive years. We owe it to ourselves and our loved ones to be as fulfilled and thrilled as possible every day so we are always ready to share our best selves with each other. There is so much in life that is uncontrollable, but our happiness doesn't have to be, nor do our careers. We can have all the control. Every damn bit of it. The sooner we realize that, the better off everyone will be.

I cannot do anything to make you more creative, but I hope that I can put you in the right frame of mind so that when you're ready to unleash that creativity, you will succeed. We are often told we have to make a choice—settle and do something tolerable to make money, or follow our passion with the expectation that we will be poor. There are still people out there who believe that it's a rare person who loves his or her job. That's bullshit. Our choices are infinite when we understand today's digital environment, as are our opportunities. We just have to find the courage to reach out and make them. You're going to hear the stories of people who were scared, just like you. Who had obligations, just like you. Who were told they were being foolish, or reckless, or irresponsible, or immature. They did it anyway and reaped the rewards. If there's anything this book should teach you, it's that the only thing stopping you from achieving lasting career and life happiness is you.

I

GET PUMPED

1

THE PATH IS ALL YOURS

An entrepreneur is someone who finds a way.

—Shaun "Shonduras" McBride

The promise of my first business book, *Crush It!*, was to teach entrepreneurs how to monetize their passion by using social media to build a strong personal brand to attract customers and advertisers to their websites, as well as transform them into such trusted experts or entertainment figures that brands and outlets would pay them to talk, consult, and attend events. In other words, it was all about building a personal brand around your business strong enough to make you an influencer. And yet the word *influencer* doesn't appear once. The multibillion-dollar influencer marketing industry was still so new at the time, the concept hadn't crystallized when that book was published in 2009. Yet today, influencer marketing is poised to eat a real chunk of traditional marketing's lunch. Younger consumers spend increasingly less time on traditional media and more time consuming content online.

- ▶ YouTube's daily viewership is closing in on TV's 1.25 billion hours per day, as television viewership falls every year.
- ▶ One in every five minutes spent on mobile is spent on Facebook's apps and services.
- ▶ Every minute, 65,900 videos and photos are posted on Instagram.
- ▶ Over 3 billion snaps are created each day on Snapchat, where over 60 percent of ads are watched with the audio on.

Consequently, since 2009, brands have tripled the amount of money they spend on social media. With the explosion in the number of social networks available to anyone who wants to amass an audience, and vast sums of money being redirected toward those networks, influencer marketing has become a legitimate monetization strategy for anyone building an online profile, which means pretty much anyone in business.

How legitimate? The top-grossing YouTubers earned a combined $70 million in 2016. Many fit a certain type—several are gamer dudes, for example—but Lilly Singh is a rapper-comedian who features Punjabi culture in her videos, Rosanna Pansino is a baker, and Tyler Oakley is an LGBTQ activist. In the past, the top-grossing list has also included dancing violinist Lindsey Stirling and makeup artist Michelle Phan. The most popular Instagrammers can earn seven figures per year from their social-media efforts alone. Even with only a thousand followers, an entry-level Instagrammer could earn about $5,000 per year with just two posts a week, and ten thousand followers could net almost $20,000 per year. Again, that's with just two posts per week; imagine the earnings if that Instagrammer posted more frequently. Let's think about that. The median salary for US employees is about $51,000. You can earn that as an office manager, or you can earn the same amount running your own business built around something you love more than anything else in the world. Want to play it safe? You can work as an office manager, go home, and then earn an extra $10,000 a year on Twitch letting people watch you play and comment on your favorite video game, because you really are that good at it. Or use YouTube to share insanely cool science experiments. Or post pictures on Instagram of your pet hedgehogs wearing tiny hats. Thanks to the proliferation of platforms and the migration of TV and magazine viewers to the Internet, there is room for many, many more experts and personalities to create a lucrative, sustainable ecosystem that promotes and grows their businesses or even side hustles.

It's a great time to be a fashion model, for example. There was a time when there was room for only a handful of superstars to see themselves featured in editorial fashion spreads and on the runways. Then there were maybe a thousand in the middle getting steady commercial work in print and TV. The rest found themselves at the bottom, scraping by doing catalog and promotional work. But the Internet has opened a floodgate of opportunity for anyone willing to hustle to grow a fan base through blogs and video channels to attract the attention of the hundreds of thousands of brands eager to spend money supporting popular, good-looking, fashionable people by branded content and advertising. Not only that, people blessed with model good looks—or even just blessed with angle and filter savvy—don't actually have to model to get paid. The huge shift in attention to social media means that beautiful people are no longer beholden to the magazines or talent agencies or anyone, really, to make money off their looks. They can look fabulous every day on their own platforms while engaging with a steadily growing audience, and brands will come begging for exposure. Just ask Brittany Xavier (see page 229).

We often define an influencer as someone who garners such a big audience on social media that brands offer to pay that person to attend events, take selfies with products, or talk about services. Brands have paid the famous people of the Internet billions of dollars to be their endorsers, sponsors, promoters, and product placers. Product placement is a natural fit with the YouTube and Instagram crowd, but it can leave the motorcycle-king bloggers or raspberry-jam-queen podcasters—those who might not feel photogenic or charismatic enough for constant selfies or video—feeling as if their options for growing their influence and building revenue streams are limited to selling ad space. I'm here to tell you, they are not. You just have to be smart and strategic about how you use your content. Look, I've been paid to write books and speak on national and international stages, and I've earned enough to make the kind of investments that could pay out for generations. However, I have not made one penny because an energy drink company paid me to say, "This is my secret to working eighteen hours a day."

I'm an entrepreneur who built a $150 million media company in part because of my personal brand, which I developed by first creating valuable content that grew my influence. That's one way to crush it. By all means, though, go ahead and make money over time by running ads, for example by selling ad space to a candy bar company. As your star rises, you could get paid $10,000 for placing a candy bar on your table while you work. But for God's sake, don't stop there. That's where you start. Don't leave money on the table because you don't realize how much bigger you can get. How big? The Internet is an entrepreneur's oyster, and you can use its pearly platforms to build a personal brand so powerful that the world is not only willing to pay you for your products or services or to promote other people's products and services, but also it might even be willing to pay you to just be you. To me, that is when you've become a true influencer. At its height, influencer marketing is reality TV 2.0. I want you to think of yourself as tomorrow's newest star.

You the entrepreneur are no different from the organic mac-and-cheese brand that branches out into cheddar cheese crackers and chicken noodle soup. The brand was never about organic mac and cheese; it was about organic comfort food. You're the expectant mom who starts a pregnancy podcast and then writes a book on raising kids suffering from anxiety. You're the home cook with a beautiful Instagram stream who starts a podcast on canning and gets invited to write a column about urban gardening in a national magazine. You're the boy who started a wine blog that wasn't actually about wine but about making a name for himself as the person who could show other businesses better ways to communicate and sell. The home cook's Instagram isn't about food but about building her influence in the healthy-lifestyle category. The mom's podcast on pregnancy is just the patty of a parenthood burger.

Your personal brand can get you all the fixings you want. Its outsize importance in today's business world means stardom is no longer limited to the most beautiful or telegenic among us; the field is open to many, many more players. It also means that most entrepreneurs still have lots of room to ratchet up their game to become influencers. I'm watching you out there, and it's shocking to me how many entrepreneurs trap themselves into boxes of their own making, even though they have so much more power than they did before.

Let's say you're killing it on Twitter. What are you going to do the day you realize you're tired of Twitter? What are you going to do if Twitter disappears? What if you're the country's favorite beekeeper and you develop a deadly allergy to bees? It's a matter of survival to think beyond your current successes and constantly look for ways to create new ones so that you're never limited to any one platform or even one topic. How do you do that? By creating a personal brand so powerful that it transcends platforms, products, and even your passion.

Take cultural icon Julie Andrews,[*] the rosy-cheeked star of multiple Broadway and Hollywood masterpieces like *Camelot*, *The Sound of Music*, and *Mary Poppins*. Her entire career—her entire identity—was built on the soaring soprano voice that made her a household name. "I thought . . . my voice was what I am." Then about twenty years ago, she had surgery to remove precancerous cysts on her vocal cords. When she awoke, the cysts were gone, but so was her voice. But because she was Julie Andrews, that wasn't the end of her career. She has

---

* Betcha didn't know I love Broadway.

since written dozens of children's books, starred in the blockbuster movie series *The Princess Diaries*, and most recently, in conjunction with Jim Henson Company, produced and starred in a Netflix series that teaches arts appreciation to preschoolers.

Oprah was not just a talk show host. Muhammad Ali was not just a boxer. The Rock is not just a wrestler. A strong personal brand is your ticket to complete personal and professional freedom. I want you to become the Julie Andrews or Muhammad Ali of your industry. Of course, for this to work, you have to start with phenomenal talent. Unlike these celebrities, though, you won't need an agent to get you noticed by the right people and start making better money. In 2009, a comedian who amassed thousands of followers cracking jokes on Twitter started making real money only when she got signed by Creative Artists Agency and landed a "real job" writing jokes for David Letterman. Today, however, you don't need to write jokes for other people when the maker of M&M's, Mars, could pay you $10,000 to tweet your own M&M joke. And you don't need to sell your material to a television network to land a lucrative deal. Let's remember that back in 2009, people still used their phones *as phones*. We were still using flip cams to film our videos, and our phones hadn't metamorphosed into our televisions and movie screens. That's all changed. The Internet became the ultimate middleman, allowing every industry to go direct-to-consumer, from music and publishing to taxis and hotels. Snapchat, Instagram, and Facebook are the NBC, ABC, and CBS of our day. Your audience is waiting for you. What you need to do is figure out how you're going to become the next *Empire*.

In 2009, I was trying to get you to understand that you could make some money in the online world or use it to catapult yourself to the mainstream if that was your end goal. Today, the Internet *is* the mainstream. You are in complete control of how the world sees you, how often, and in what context. Social-media phenom John "The Fat Jewish" Ostrovsky had been on the entertainment circuit for years, signing with a record label in college and hosting a celebrity interview show on *E!*, but it wasn't until he amassed half a million followers on Instagram that he was able to parlay his comedy and performance art into a book deal, a wine label, and appearances on reality TV (which led to his gaining ten million followers on Instagram). Superstar filmmaker Casey Neistat started making online films as far back as 2003, but it was the high-quality short films and creative daily vlog he posted on YouTube that cemented his personal brand in the minds and hearts of eight million followers. With that audience, he was able to sell his company to CNN for $25 million, launch a new project there that aims to bridge "the gigantic divide" between his young-skewing audience and the mainstream news media, and become the face of a Samsung commercial that aired during the 2017 Oscars.

Personal Brands Are for Everyone

Strategically developing a personal brand through social media works brilliantly for creatives, as proven by the high number of photographers, artists, and musicians who offered to share their stories for this book when I put the call out for submissions. However, it can work for anyone in any industry who wants to put in the hustle. You no longer have to toil incognito behind someone else's name or logo until you build enough cred to strike out on your own. Of course you can, and many do, often to build up their knowledge, life experience, and savings accounts before taking that entrepreneurial leap. Several of the people interviewed for this book said that the experiences and skills they gained in their former jobs—even the ones they hated—were essential to helping them become the entrepreneurs they are today. Take, for instance, Dan Markham, who cohosts YouTube's What's Inside? channel with his son, Lincoln.

As a sales rep, oddly enough, learning how to convince doctors to use certain drugs taught me how to be a YouTuber. I would practice with the other representatives. We'd practice and practice and practice and practice and practice. I'd never been on camera before, but I feel like the camera is just like talking to one of those other drug reps or in front of the doctor. And so, my job actually helped me. I knew I wanted to be an entrepreneur, I knew I wanted to own my own business. But I was working so hard going to college and going to my day job and learning all I could from being a sales rep. And then doing all the little things on the side. And failing and succeeding. And then finally, it just kind of came together.

I'm thirty-seven, and I've been working on this since I was nineteen years old, trying to develop myself. It took all of those years for it to happen. But now I feel like I'm finally at a place where I wanted to be. It's crazy that this is where it is, but I love it.

Isn't it cool to know there is no prescribed route? If you're a project manager who'd rather be a beekeeper, for example, tomorrow—yes, *tomorrow*—you could launch a nature-oriented podcast and blog with perceptive, humorous, creative content, and amplify your voice in all kinds of arenas beyond bees. Then you could start producing how-to videos or write a book about starting in the biz, ensuring that your knowledge is passed on to the new generation of beekeepers. You'd be sharing important information and growing your personal brand at the same time. And then, you could be asked to host a special on *Animal Planet*, or *National Geographic* could call and say they want to do a feature. As your personal brand grows, you might develop a recipe for a new honey-flavored candy, lip balm, lozenge, or yogurt. You might create a new bug spray or skin regimen, or design bee-branded tote bags and gardening materials. Or you may get a direct message on Instagram from fashion model Karlie Kloss, who, it turns out, is super into bee culture, and the tagged selfie you take together not only boosts your book sales from three hundred to thirty thousand, but also it sparks the next chapter of your career. That shit is really happening. Use today's social-media platforms to develop your brand and expand your influence, and you can build a business that could continue to grow even if you never touched another hive.

That's just a hypothetical example, but you'll read lots of real ones in the following pages. This book is a celebration of all the people who have put the *Crush It!* principles to work and seen massive success in return. I want you to learn from their examples. Some represented here are my friends; many are just random people who, when given the chance, stepped up to share with you how they did it. It was nearly impossible to choose from among the inspiring stories we heard, and I wish we could have featured everyone who reached out to me and my staff. There just wasn't room.* We heard great stories from entertainers, fitness professionals, fashion bloggers, and of course, marketing consultants—people you might expect to be crushing it on social media—but we also heard from a dentist, a financial planner, a dog trainer, a LEGO convention planner, and a quick-lube oil-change business owner, among scores of others. Many started out young and single, but some already had kids when they decided to double down and crush it. Several gave up lucrative jobs to devote themselves to their passion. What this should tell you is that if you're not crushing it, it's not because you're too old or poor or have too many other responsibilities. It's because you haven't fully committed to making the leap yet. You're making excuses, like, "Gary makes it seem so easy, yet this is really almost impossible." It's not, actually, but you can't half-ass this. It will require big risks. It will take all your mental capacity, your time, and your leisure. **You're going to eat shit for a long time,** but I promise, the sacrifices will be worthwhile. I also promise that once you've developed a robust personal brand, you will be able

---

* Which is why we created a *Medium* page called "Crushing It," where we publish stories and celebrate people who are using *Crush It!* principles to achieve personal and professional success. Come check it out at https://medium.com/crushingit.

to enjoy as much or as little leisure as you want—because you will be entirely in control of your own life.

Don't look for a nine-step program to success here, though. I can't give you one. The principles are universal; the path is all yours. I will give you examples of how to use the platforms, as will the people who shared their stories with us. But they're just examples, not commands. You can do it my way, or you can do it your way. Chart your path in the spirit of *Crush It!*, if not by the letter. You just have to make the choice to actually do it. I am so tired of excuses. Why not try something new? Be optimistic, exhibit patience, shut your mouth, and execute.

The most exciting thing about the business world we live in is that it is still in its infancy. There is so much room to succeed here. Unbelievably, a lot of you still seem to balk at experimenting with new up-and-coming platforms. You don't want to waste your time if it turns out to be just another fast-fading trend, but then you wonder why influencers like the ones you're about to meet are succeeding so much better than you are. That disconnect is what gives entrepreneurs like you such an early advantage. Now there is even more opportunity to cash in on your passion than there was back then. Grab your spot, make your mark, and start living in the *Crush It!* universe.

HOW I'M CRUSHING IT

Amy Schmittauer, Savvy Sexy Social

IG: @SCHMITTASTIC

Amy Schmittauer became an Internet sensation because she got picked last to be a bridesmaid. It was 2007, and though she was the last one chosen, she wanted to be the favorite, so she thought about what she could do to make the bride feel special and came up with the idea of making a video with one of the other bridesmaids. She had fun making it and was sure the bride would appreciate the gesture, but it wasn't until she played it at the rehearsal dinner that she realized the power of the medium. The bride wasn't the only one crying over the video; the whole room was moved to tears.

"I got hooked immediately. I loved the idea of telling a story and being able to have an emotional control over an audience. It engages all the senses at once."

The video Amy had made for the wedding was burned onto a DVD. She was thrilled, however, to discover the existence of online platforms onto which she could upload videos and share them. She started filming pieces of her life, taught herself how to edit, and displayed the results on YouTube. The process became her creative outlet.

In the meantime, while majoring in political science at The Ohio State University, thinking she might want to go to law school, she managed to get a dream job at a law firm, where she eventually got involved in lobbying, fundraising, and public policy. But she also became known as the person who knew how to edit videos and could help you figure out the privacy settings on your Facebook page, which would not have been remarkable in Silicon Valley but was unusual in Ohio at the time. It was friends living on the West Coast who informed her that social-media management was a real job. And she thought, *I could get paid to do this?*

That's when the side hustle started. After getting home from her day job, sometimes as late as seven p.m., she'd buckle down to the freelance work. The first small businesses she approached were already overwhelmed by all the content they had to create for Facebook and Twitter, and now here's this person telling them they had to make videos, too? They didn't want to hear it. Amy realized that the only way she was going to get small companies to take her seriously was to show them why social mattered. She got her first client, a local sustainable food magazine, by sending an e-mail explaining that although she didn't have any formal social-media experience, she was sure she could help them develop their brand. **Oh, and she was willing to do it for free.** It didn't take a lot of convincing for them to take her on as their social-media manager.

She had been working the side job along with her full-time job at the law firm for three or four months when Lewis Howes, also from Ohio, who was by then making a name for himself with LinkedIn (see page 34), suggested they meet. He didn't find her through the work she was doing for the sustainable food magazine; he had noticed the photo and video blogging she was doing on You-Tube and other social-media sites, and wanted to know more about what she was doing. They met over burgers in the spring of 2010, and he gave her two pieces of advice if she wanted to start getting paying clients:

1. Go to Las Vegas and attend BlogWorld, the new-media conference where the leaders in blogging, podcasting, and video content creation gather to talk about their craft and businesses.

   Not a problem. The magazine had already helped her purchase a badge.

2. Read *Crush It!*, by Gary Vaynerchuk.

   That was easy, too. Amy went to the library and picked up a copy. She read it, and that's when she knew she wasn't going to become a lawyer after all.

I would have been happy to do this as a side job for-ever. I didn't know that I could be powerful enough to make this happen. *Crush It!* made me able to envision what my future could look like. I'd been thinking that I first needed to become a prestigious company to get other businesses to hire me, and I didn't give enough credit to the fact that I was already being watched, asked for advice, trusted, and considered a mini-thought leader because of the personal brand I'd developed through the videos about my life.

It made me realize how important personal branding is to growing a business, and I was already doing it without even knowing it. So maybe I was further ahead than I thought! Maybe I could turn this thing I was do-ing for fun into something else by simply leveraging what I knew really well—how to use video, how to talk to a camera like it's a person—and then craft the mes-saging for a very specific type of person. It was the only fire I ever really needed to hit the ground running because I knew what to do at that point.

Now she knew that social-media management wasn't going to be her sector of the online world. She was going to go after vlog and personal brand consulting. And she was going to ask for what she was worth.

Obviously, the definition of devaluing yourself is work-ing for free, but I also think I would have stayed too low in my pricing because of how much it was deval-ued as an industry in the beginning. *Crush It!* allowed me to wrap my mind around the fact that my skill was a major, major asset, both in marketing and customer service for businesses. That's what made me a lot more confident in my pricing and monetizing on my terms. And my confidence, believing that I'm worth more, has helped me get paid much more over my career. I just kept taking the chance, because I knew I was doing good work.

She started her vlog, Savvy Sexy Social, "to end the misery that small businesses were going through." By the time she quit her job in the beginning of 2011, she had gotten some paying clients, but the switch from salaried employee to freelancer was still a huge risk. She moved in with her boyfriend, got rid of her car, and did everything she could to keep her overhead low. She was prepared for it to take months to bring in new clients, but all the work she'd done in the wings—getting people to know and trust her by talking about her work, attending Blog-World, following up with her network, and being diligent with building relationships—paid off. She had paying clients within a few weeks. (To make sure she stood firm on her prices, for a while she created a separate virtual assistant e-mail and negotiated for herself under a different persona.)

While continuing to teach on Savvy Sexy Social, which has over seventy-five thousand subscribers and has received over five million views, Amy has written a best-selling book, created a series of online courses on vlogging for business, and started a second successful video marketing business, and she still presents keynotes all over the world. She's newly married (hello, Mrs. Landino!), she has a cute dog, and business is thriving. By any measure, she's crushing it, yet she's reluctant to congratulate herself.

I've had a hard time fully appreciating what I've accomplished at any point. I understand that I am in complete control, and that's an overwhelming feeling because it means you could always be doing more, and it means you might not be doing enough. Amazing things happen, and then there's a day when I wake up and it's a bad day and it's like, *I'm failing*. I never got close to quitting, but there were days when I was thinking, *Are you really cut out for this?* I was my own biggest challenge. I didn't take the time to be grateful and give myself the respect that I had come so far. It sounds fluffy, but I had to start sitting down and reflecting on a weekly, daily, monthly basis on what I did well, and be happy with that, and remember it the next day, because it's going to be hard every day. Waking up and knowing the challenges will come—and they do—I still wouldn't change a thing. I know I chose my right path, and I love continuing to follow it no matter what.

Amy has a great story, right? I love how she scratched her own itch. I love how she successfully channeled all her energy into creating an incredible brand, and yet despite having accomplished so much, continues to navigate and doesn't let up for one second. She is the embodiment of patience and tenacity, as are all the other people we interviewed for this book. I can't wait for you to meet them.

2

WHAT (STILL) MATTERS

Before we explore which platform you should select to support your pillar of content, I want to remind you that even a well-designed pillar will fall if it isn't set in a solid base. What usually hamstrings entrepreneurs isn't merely the mistakes they make when executing their vision, but the mistakes they make before they even get started. While it can be hard to pinpoint why some influencers build attractive, lucrative personal brands that succeed beyond their wildest expectations, it's not hard to figure out why so many who attempt to do it fail. In general, it's because they're putting their energies into the wrong things. They care, but not enough about what really matters. And what really matters is a pretty short list: intent, authenticity, passion, patience, speed, work, and attention.

Intent

In business, the how matters, of course, but the why matters just as much. Maybe more. Why do you want to be an entrepreneur?

To share your knowledge?

To help people?

To build something that leaves a legacy?

To make a good income to give yourself and your family financial security and breathing room?

To have fun with a creative outlet?

To create community?

All of these are great reasons for building a business and becoming
an influencer.

Notice what isn't on the list?

With entrepreneurship becoming so trendy, a lot of people are
calling themselves entrepreneurs who really aren't. They should call
themselves *wantrepreneurs* instead, and I wish they'd do this before
they ruin the reputation of real entrepreneurs the same way unscru-
pulous brokers ruined how some feel about real estate agents or the
way ambulance chasers and media hounds tarnished our opinion of
lawyers. (And I wish they'd rename themselves before they waste a
lot of time and potentially money). I promise you that getting into
this game for the gold is the quickest path to long-term failure. When
your intent is coming from the wrong place, customers may still do
business with you if they have no other option (an increasingly rare
situation), but they won't tell others to. By definition, an influencer
engenders positive word of mouth. If you don't care enough to induce
others to rave about you, all you're doing is holding a spot for someone
who really does care, the one who will waltz in and displace you.

This book features entrepreneurs at all levels of financial success
and all stages of influence, but those currently at the pinnacle of both
share three characteristics:

▶ A commitment to service
▶ A desire to provide value
▶ A love of teaching

A number were inspired to create their products after unsuccessfully searching for those products themselves, sure that if they needed them, others did, too. They started teaching when all they found when looking for mentorship or inspiration were overpriced online courses that took up their time but didn't offer anything truly useful. When creating their content, they vowed to take the completely opposite approach by offering solid content and real value. By their own admission, most didn't start out as the most knowledgeable in their fields, and they certainly weren't the most polished. But what they lacked in experience they made up for in earnestness, honesty, and humor. Every day their podcasts, photos, videos, and blog posts improved, drawing their audiences back again and again. They gave, gave, gave, gave, and gave some more, often for free. And customers came back again and again. Was it because they liked getting stuff for free? Sure, everyone does. But if a product stinks, even free won't make up for your customers' disappointment. In addition, a stinky product blows any chance you might have had to earn your customers' trust and loyalty. No one comes back for products or advice that doesn't work.

Now, I'm the least naïve person you've ever met. Some may hate me for saying this, but I don't believe that most of these people give so much away because they're so goddamn selfless. They're human, which means that, like everyone else, they have their own selfish wants and needs. But I also believe they are humans who fall into the 51 percent. That is, if your nature is at least 51 percent altruistic and only 49 percent selfish, you have a real shot at breaking out, because the vast majority of people are 70 to 99 percent selfish. Could you use altruism as a tactic? Sure, but altruism is not the kind of thing you can fake for very long. All the people I've known who've tried have been able to grow only so big before they were financially and/or emotionally broke. I'll bet some of the people mentioned in this book started out using altruism as a tactic, and they were good at it because it came naturally. Then they noticed that consumers react pretty strongly when they feel that you give a shit about them, which gave them the incentive to play up that side of themselves rather than fight it, which is what most of us rocked in the cradle of capitalism have always been taught to do. Breaking the money-first rule is also how I got to where I am. I have never cared about the money. I do, however, care deeply, obsessively, about my legacy. I want the world to mourn me when I die, not just for being a decent human being, but for building something tremendous and predicting where the future of business lay. And then I want to fucking own the afterlife. Being good and generous and giving a crap is the only thing that will get me either of those goals. Three out of ten people don't like me the first time they catch me online or hear me talk because they think I'm full of shit, and that my habit of giving so much away for free, whether it's time, advice, or mentorship, is just a gateway to making money. They don't believe anyone really cares that much. I do, though, which is why the majority of my haters eventually change their minds if they give me a fair hearing.

There are a scary number of people who say they're starting their business because they want to make the world a better place yet reveal themselves as frauds and hypocrites in answering one or two direct questions about their model. There are also a scary number of people who are so cynical that they can't believe anyone does anything without expecting something in return. I acknowledge the duality of human nature, including my own. I want to buy the New York Jets (let's be honest; I'm addicted to the process of trying to buy the New York Jets), which means I do what I do so I can make a lot of money. At the same time, I love how it feels to make a positive impact on people's lives, which means I do what I do so I can help other entrepreneurs succeed. Embracing these two truths and combining them in my daily actions is why I win. It's also why I leave ungodly amounts of money on the table. For example, many influencers, including some you'll meet here, sell online courses. Courses can provide a hefty revenue stream, and done right, they can be incredible resources. I choose not to because I'm concerned that, once I put a monetary value on what I know, I'll feel obligated to reserve my best stuff for the people willing to pay. It would create a conflict of interest that would go against everything I want my brand to be about. I do publish books, but other than an occasional personal anecdote, there's no information in them that I have not discussed in a public, free forum somewhere else. For anyone with the time and inclination to do the online digging, the information is there for the taking, albeit sometimes in a less expansive, less detailed format. These books exist to save people time and to provide a portable resource people can easily refer to.

In every decision I make, I consider the balance I'm willing to strike between selfishness and selflessness, with my selfish side often getting short shrift in the short term. I'm fine with waiting a few more years than I might otherwise have to to buy the Jets if it means I get to live with a clear conscience and the knowledge that I haven't sacrificed my legacy. You may make a different decision. The truth is, you don't have to be as altruistic as I am to win big; in a world where the standard is pretty much nothing, you have to be just altruistic enough. But believe me, if your every interaction and transaction is predicated on what you think you're going to get out of it, nothing in this book will work for you. Consider yourself warned.

At the other end of the spectrum, it's interesting how often the product actually seems beside the point to many of the successful entrepreneurs interviewed for this book. Their passion isn't entirely tied up in the protein powder, the training technique, or the beauty products. For many of them, to borrow the words of graphic design and branding instructor Jenna Soard (IG: @youcanbrand), founder of You Can Brand, their "truest love is watching the 'ahas' go off in people's minds." It's in seeing how their product or service makes others feel, in helping customers solve problems, achieve more, or feel better about themselves. In short, the source of their success lies in how much they

CARE.

Still the best marketing strategy ever.

HOW I'M CRUSHING IT

Lewis Howes, School of Greatness

IG: @LEWISHOWES

Lewis Howes knows the sound of a broken dream. For him, it was the snap of his wrist as he slammed against a wall during his second game as a professional arena football player. An All-American football player and decathlete, Lewis at first refused to accept that the injury meant he'd never play professional sports again. For six months as he recuperated from extensive surgery in a full-arm cast on his sister's couch in Ohio, he held out hope that he'd recover enough to resume his athletic career. But after another year of trying and failing to rebuild the strength he'd once had in his arm, he had to accept that it was over. For a lot of people, it would have felt like the end. He'd already survived childhood sexual abuse and been bullied in school, where he had struggled to keep up due to dyslexia. Sports had been his refuge and his salvation, and he'd dropped out of college to try out for the NFL. Now, despite all his efforts, he was left with nothing—no degree, no skills, and no money. And it was 2008, when even people with ample amounts of all three couldn't find a job.

What Lewis did have, thanks to his athletic training, was a belief in himself. He started pondering the question, "What could I create if I could create anything in the world?" He already knew what it felt like to get paid to do something he loved, so there was no question of taking any old corporate job he could get. But he needed to do *something*, because after so many months of living on her couch rent free, his sister was getting impatient.

A mentor suggested he get on LinkedIn. Lewis realized that the platform gave him direct access to lots of successful people, people who might be able to lead him to opportunities or at least explain to him how they had gotten to where they were.

"All I ever wanted to do was be around inspiring people that I could learn from." He spent the next year, eight hours or so a day, connecting with local business leaders, inviting them to lunch and conducting informational interviews to learn more about how they'd achieved their success. Thinking he might be a natural fit for a job in the sports world, he'd at first reached out to a number of sports executives. As one person connected him to another person, who then suggested he meet with another, his circle grew wider. As he learned more about LinkedIn's possibilities, he optimized his profile, which then led to bigger and bigger influencers agreeing to meet with him. By the end of 2009, he had thirty-five thousand connections.

At the time, Tweetups—in-person gatherings of Twitter users around a common cause—were a popular networking venue.

"I went to a couple and I thought, *Hmmm, I'm building this following on LinkedIn. Why don't I do a LinkedIn meetup?*" So he did one in St. Louis, where he had once gone to private boarding school. Three hundred fifty people attended, and thanks to selling a few sponsorship tables, he earned about a thousand dollars.

"So I was like, *Hmmm, why don't I see if I can do another event and charge five dollars at the door?*" He did, and he made money off the entry fee as well as the sponsorships.

"And then I was like, *Hmmm, I'm building a relationship with these venues. What if I asked for a 10 percent commission on the food and bar sales from these networking events?*" They said yes.

In short order, Lewis was bringing in a couple thousand dollars a month, enough to finally get off his sister's couch and move into his own apartment, the cheapest one he could find, a little one-bedroom for $495 per month in Columbus, Ohio.

People were astounded. How was he pulling this off? He didn't have a real job, he didn't have a college degree, and yet he was bringing big influencers together all over the country and being asked to speak at conferences. All through LinkedIn. They started asking if he could show them how to use the platform for their businesses, too. And Lewis thought, *Hmmm*.

Lewis started teaching other entrepreneurs and businesspeople how to optimize their profile and reach out to potential clients, investors, or whomever they needed.

"I think because I came with energy and passion, I attracted opportunities. I attracted people to come to these events. I became passionate about teaching, because no one else was talking about LinkedIn the way I was. I made it fun when LinkedIn is very boring for a lot of people."

Not long afterward, he found out that an entrepreneur named Gary Vaynerchuk would be having a signing for his new book, *Crush It!*, in St. Louis. Lewis reached out and offered to help promote the event on LinkedIn.* Given that he was helping promote the book, it made sense to read it. It was a long time ago, and he remembers very few of the details today, except for one chapter: Care.

> I never felt like I was smart. I never felt like I had the intelligence, or the skills, or the experience, or the credentials. I didn't have any of that. So when I read that word, I thought, *Yes!* I needed to continue to deepen my level of care! When I would meet with these influencers, I would never ask for advice. I would just say, "I'm so curious to hear your story about how you became successful." And at the end of that I would say, "What's the biggest challenge you have in your business, or your career, or your life right now?" and listen. And they would tell me everything they needed. I said, "You need a sales guy? I've got three of the top ones right here. You need a programmer? I've got this person. You need a designer? I met one last week. He was great." I just became this connector to all the most successful people. I never asked for a job. I never asked for business. That one-word chapter confirmed that when we show up and we add value and we care, then we can learn how to make money around it later. But show up with value first. That is how I built the last decade of my life.

Lewis was already teaching himself to be entrepreneurial and making a little money, but now, inspired, he really put

---

* He later mentioned it on his blog in a post he wrote dedicated to improving my LinkedIn performance: https://lewishowes.com/featured-articles/13-ways-gary-vaynerchuk-should-be-crushing-it-on-linkedin.

on the gas. *Crush It!* said you had to be niche, so he decided he wasn't going to be "the social-media guy" like everyone else in 2008–2009; he was going to be the LinkedIn guy. *Crush It!* said work fifteen-to-sixteen-hour days, so that's what he did. "I was working my ass off." He built up his expertise until every social-media conference was booking him as the LinkedIn speaker. He also got creative.

> I started approaching venues, which were mostly restaurants and bars, and built a relationship with either the manager or the owner. I'd try thinking about how I could make my event valuable for them. How could I care for their biggest need, their biggest challenges? So I started asking, "What is the night you make the least amount of money?" And they would answer "Tuesday night" or "Wednesday night" or whatever it was, and I'd say, "OK. I'm going to bring you five hundred people on that night, because I want to make every night a profitable night for you, not just the weekends. And I'm going to bring new business leaders, a new audience of quality people to your business."

Lewis did, and what was once these venues' worst night became their biggest night. From then on, they were willing to let Lewis host events any time he asked. He did, but he also started taking bigger risks.

"I just started to go for it and ask for what I wanted, even if I thought it wasn't going to work. I started asking for 20 percent commission off food and bar, as opposed to 10 percent. I charged twenty dollars at the door instead of five. And I started charging more for sponsorships."

Because Lewis was bringing so much value to the venues, the sponsors, and the event attendees, all were more than happy to pay a higher price for Lewis's services. In one year, he hosted twenty events around the country.

He branched out into other service products, and in two years, the company was bringing in over $2.5 million in sales. But despite the success, after a few years, Lewis was ready to do something new. "I became less passionate. There's only so much I can talk about how to add the right photograph and optimize your LinkedIn profile." He sold his business and got started on his next project, School of Greatness, a podcast that shares inspiring stories, messages, and practical advice from some of the biggest athletes, celebrities, and business minds in the world.

Since its inception in 2013, School of Greatness has been downloaded tens of millions of times and makes a regular appearance in the iTunes podcast Top 50. In 2015, Lewis published his *New York Times* best seller, *The School of Greatness*. He continues to coach, attend speaking events, and contribute articles to major media outlets. And while Lewis still loves and uses LinkedIn, he has also focused his efforts on other platforms that drive the most traffic, downloads, and sales and help him continue to build his audience. At this point, the only thing holding him back is that he's just one man, so he has hired a stellar team to help him run all aspects of the business, from podcast editing to Facebook ads to customer support.

"I feel like the luckiest guy in the world. I had to learn the skills I needed and become competent enough to match my confidence, but the thing that surprises me the most is learning that it's not about how much you know; it's about how much you care. We can create anything we want to if we have the passion, the energy, the hustle, and commitment to our vision. If I had been a jerk all along the way and I didn't care about people, there's no chance

I would have been able to do this. If you show up with that energy and intensity every single day, good things are going to happen.

███████████████████████████████████████

Authenticity

Your intent will be reflected in your authenticity. You will be a thousand times more successful if you wake up eager to share and create something because you believe the world will enjoy it rather than because you have calculated that this is what you need to do to become an Instagram celebrity. Authenticity is a welcome relief to consumers who live in a society where they constantly feel that they're being taken advantage of or hearing only parts of the whole story. Don't try to fake it. Eventually you'll be shown for who you are. Instead, figure out how to use the modern platforms—Instagram, Snapchat, You-Tube, and all the others we'll cover in this book—to give away that good stuff you've got, whether it's your incredible fashion sense, your hilarious brand of comedy, your innovative team-building strategies, or your stunning flower-arrangement ideas. Figure out the best platforms to showcase your true self, your craft, your joy, and your love for what you do. The more authentic you are, the more people will be willing to forgive your inevitable mistakes and stumbles.

I mentioned above that a good chunk of my audience is converts, people who thought I was just a blowhard until they realized that my message was consistent and that I kept being proven right. Even if people don't like me, few ever doubt that I'm for real. There are three things working to my advantage in this regard: number one, I genuinely don't give a shit what people think, which allows me complete freedom to do and say what I want; number two, I care immensely what everyone thinks and will spend an insane amount of time responding to skeptics who take the time to tweet or comment their criticism, to help them see where I'm coming from; and number three, which might be more important than numbers one or two, I always respect my audience. I believe in people's intuition, and I believe that most are very good at sniffing out hypocrisy and opportunism. Exploiting your consumers because you think they're dumb—for example, selling them an expensive online course that's mostly fluff and nonsense—is, well, dumb. You may count on people's ignorance to make a lot of money in the short term, but you will be in a mess of manure the minute your customers find out you're taking advantage of them. That goes for corporations as well as personal brands. All it takes is a single viral video of a customer getting forcibly dragged off a plane to expose a company's crooked policies. When you disrespect your customer, you're one social-media post away from having your whole business tumble down around you. I have no interest in taking that kind of risk, and neither should you.

HOW I'M CRUSHING IT

Lauryn Evarts, The Skinny Confidential

IG: @THESKINNYCONFIDENTIAL

Lauryn is the willowy, sassy bombshell behind and in front of the lifestyle site The Skinny Confidential. When asked to describe her passion, she says it's about building community and bringing women together. But she also chafes a bit at the question.

I can't stand when people are like passion, passion, passion. It's so much more than passion. Execute. I see a lot of people in my generation talking about ideas and saying what they're going to do. I hate talking about what I'm going to do. I don't think I talked about The Skinny Confidential once for the whole year I was building it until it was here. Because I like to show.

That's probably why her father, also an entrepreneur, thought to give her a copy of *Crush It!* for Christmas the year it came out. At the time, Lauryn was still a TV broadcasting and theater major at San Diego State. She was bartending, teaching Pure Barre and Pilates, attending class, and getting bored out of her mind. A creative, independent spirit, she felt that college was a waste of time, yet with no alternative in mind, she felt she had no choice but to do what was expected and get a degree. Along the way, however, she had noticed something that piqued her interest. With *Crush It!* fresh in her head, an idea started to form.

There were not a lot of platforms online that were inspiring women to be unapologetically themselves. There are a lot of men like Gary and Tony Robbins and Tim Ferriss, all these strong amazing men, and I didn't see a woman in that space. I wanted to create one. And it wouldn't just be about me, me, me and the outfit I was wearing, but a place where I could bring models and moms and everyday women together to connect and share their secrets. I wanted to provide value, which is something I definitely learned in *Crush It!*

Lauryn used her iPhone notes and a binder to collect a tremendous list of ideas for content. Then, although she was dead broke, she hired a Web developer, paying him in ten fifty-dollar installments. For a year, she refined her craft and built her credibility, continuing to teach and earning her license online as a fitness and nutrition specialist. "Another thing that *Crush It!* said that resonated for me was, 'Always put your money back into your business.' So, I was like, work, work, work for tips and then put it back right into The Skinny Confidential. And then work, work, work for tips and then right back to The Skinny Confidential. I had zero dollars in my bank account for the longest time."

When she finally did launch, she kept her content narrowly tailored to health-related topics. "Find that niche that you're so good at and ride it, and ride it, and ride it until you can slowly expand out." In retrospect, she might have been able to start diversifying her brand within three months, but her brutal schedule would have made that difficult.

I would shoot all my photos from 2:00 to 3:30, bartend from 4:00 to 12:00, come home, write my blog post from 12:00 to 2:00, wake up, teach Pure Barre, teach Pilates, go to school, rinse and repeat, five days a week. And then on the weekend, I would do Instagram, Twitter, Facebook, and the e-mails and all the other little stuff that comes with it.

Slowly, methodically, she started expanding the scope of her brand into other categories: wellness, beauty, home décor, and clothes. But she didn't make a penny for two-and-a-half years. "The biggest mistake I see influencers make is, they'll work with every brand on the planet. It's all about how many brands can they work with, not about the audience, not about the readership. I see no longevity there. I'm more focused on building my own brand than other people's brands."

She finally monetized after being approached by a brand that she wore all the time anyway, and today she earns "definitely a very good amount," which translates to enough to provide a comfortable life, as well as employ a graphic designer, an assistant, a project manager, an editor, a photographer, and a back-end developer to help her with the day-to-day operations of the business. But she continues to turn down brands every single day, even offers of $10,000 to $15,000 to collaborate for a single blog post.

Nothing was off-limits on The Skinny Confidential: "Storytelling is so underrated." Lauryn wrote about essential oils and diet tips, but also boob jobs and Botox. She began introducing new characters from her life, mining her relationships for deeper content and fresh stories to share with her readers. Her beloved grandmother, known as The Nanz, became a fixture on the site, giving Lauryn a way to offer an unexpected perspective on her chosen themes. She unveiled her boyfriend, Michael, when they became engaged; the blog now has a whole Michael-dedicated space called Him, and the couple produces a podcast together.

Naturally, readers were privy to all the details of Lauryn's engagement and wedding. But they've also been invited to share the darker moments. Lauryn's sad, tender ode to The Nanz following the matriarch's unexpected death invited a flood of empathetic replies. When jaw surgery left her face grossly swollen for two years, Lauryn, who admits that until then "I led with my looks," showed the pictures and talked about how the disfigurement affected her self-esteem. Readers raced to support her when she shared the story of how she had listened, stunned and hurt, as two brand executives, unknowingly still connected to her by conference line, sneered at and ridiculed her following what she thought had been a promising phone call. The moment also gave her a chance to explore the hypocrisy of brands who claimed to empower and champion women, but only so long as those women fit a certain mold.

> I took all my hurt and I put it into this blog post. And I could not believe the response. Women from all over the world were writing in with stories about how they had heard someone talking about them or been bullied or put themselves out there and been bashed for it. It was really cool to be able to bring everyone together and lift each other up.
>
> Everyone says put yourself out there, be your authentic self, but when your authentic self is not what they like, they talk back. It was a very weird experience. But instead of silencing me, I'm just going to continue to put myself out there even more. And I hope that I responded in a way that can make me a good role model if my readers, especially younger girls, ever find themselves in a situation like that. If I can change someone's mind about being catty . . . if I can use the platform to call that out and say there's nothing cool about being mean, whether it's cyberbullying or bullying or talking shit about someone, then that's a good goal.

While it's unfortunate that she didn't document that first year when she was gathering her ideas and strategizing the trajectory of her business, in her case the process does seem to have sharpened her ideas so that she wasted less time and was able to act more purposefully once she did launch. She is an admirable model of speed and patience.

> This is something that I've been working on for six years every single day, seven days a week. There's been no day off. If I'm on vacation, I'm working. And I still have so much work to do. I just did what Gary said in *Crush It!*, which is constantly hitting it day after day, never giving up, keeping my blinders on, focusing on my own shit, and really, really doing me. Doing me to the best of my ability. *Crush It!*, and his other books too, allowed me to just be who I am and not be sorry about it.

Passion

I know many people working in jobs that make them heaps of money who aren't happy, but I don't know anyone who works around their passion every day who isn't loving life. As I said earlier, I could take some shortcuts to make more money and thus shorten the time it takes for me to meet my goal of buying the Jets—but I don't, because those things wouldn't make me happy. I'd rather wait and get there on my own terms. We're on this earth for only a short time, and the bulk of our adult days are spent at work. It's worth taking the steps necessary to make sure those hours are as rewarding, productive, and enjoyable as possible.

Every one of the people interviewed for this book agreed that there's no point in trying to be an entrepreneur without passion. Your business can't be just a job; it has to be a calling. Andy Frisella, founder of nutrition and fitness brands Supplement Superstores and 1ˢᵗ Phorm, explained it best:

> You're going to go through a time where you're not going to make any money. It's not going to be a week, it's not going to be a month, it's not going to be one year. It's going to be years. And during that time, if you don't love what you do, it's going to be very hard to stick it out. That is something that people don't understand when they hear, "Follow your passion." They hear rainbows, unicorns, bullshit. But the truth of it is that it's important, because if you don't enjoy what you're doing, you're going to be that much more likely to quit when shit's hard.

When you're passionate about what you're offering the world, whether it's a sales training method or vintage toys, the quality of both your product and your content will more likely be what it needs to be to get noticed, valued, and talked about. Interestingly, many of the people we interviewed pointed out that you don't even have to be passionate about the product or service you're offering. What's imperative is that you are passionate about giving. That's what Shaun "Shonduras" McBride discovered. Before developing his massively successful personal brand on Snapchat, he sold jewelry online. The guy was a skater and snowboarder; he had little interest in jewelry per se. But after reading *Crush It!* in college, he decided to sell jewelry to test the book's principles and confirm what his instincts told him were true: that engaging with customers and involving them in the development of his brand would pay dividends no matter what he sold. As you'll see later in this book, he was right.

Finally, most entrepreneurs will tell you that passion is protective, buoying you when you threaten to become overwhelmed by the stress and frustration that is a natural by-product of entrepreneurialism. **Passion is your backup generator when all your other energy sources start to sputter.** And passion keeps you happy. When you love what you do, it makes every choice easier. When you decide to keep working the nine-to-five you hate because you need the health benefits until your business takes off, when you agree to work for less money than you want because the experience will pay off later, when you eat shit—passion makes it all go down easier.

HOW I'M CRUSHING IT

Brian Wampler, Wampler Pedals

TWITTER: @WAMPLERPEDALS

Brian Wampler's parents, both commissioned sales reps, were more entrepreneurial than the average mom and dad, but they raised Brian to follow the money and do the job that paid, "regardless of whether you are passionate about it or not." So after Brian graduated high school (by the skin of his teeth) he went to work in construction. A few years later, at the age of twenty-two, he went out on his own as a remodeling subcontractor. It wasn't his passion, but it was better than working for someone else, *better* being a relative term—he *hated* what he was doing.

His real passion was guitar, in particular trying to make the guitar sound the way it did in popular songs. That sound is created through guitar pedals, small electronic boxes guitarists manipulate to create various sound effects and tones. When a friend introduced Brian to an online forum for people interested in customizing existing guitar pedals, Brian dove in.

For the next few years, I would work all day, getting home about five p.m., eat dinner and spend some time with the family, then spend the rest of the evening learning all about electronics through reading and ex-perimentation. I did this every night, not stopping until three or four a.m. . . . sometimes staying up all night and then going into work and doing it all over again.

In many of these forums, many of the questions are asked by laypersons who have no experience in electronics. Most of the people answering were either engineers or talked way over the head of the person asking the questions. When this person asked for the answer to be simplified, they were scoffed at. . . . Basically, there were artist types of people asking a question and heady engineering types refusing to dumb down the answer. I was once one of those "art-ist types" of people in the very beginning. So, once I figured everything out on my own, I simply made sure to explain things in a very easy-to-understand-and-digest manner so others could learn more easily.

(Which, incidentally, is exactly what I did for wine.)

He also started selling his own modified guitar ped-als online. That led to questions from customers, which added to the number of hours Brian spent replying to comments and answering e-mails and even phone calls. He finally published a series of e-books to consolidate all the information he was disseminating. Then he started selling DIY kits with parts and instructions for modifying particular pedals. When customers and retailers started asking him to build and sell them custom pedals, he cre-ated his own line, which is how Wampler Pedals was born. He quit the construction industry and made his liv-ing selling all these products. Demand kept rising.

Brian realized that he wasn't going to be able to keep

this pace up and invest the same amount of time in all of his products. Something was going to have to take priority. It was while trying to decide which direction to pursue, in early 2010, that he came across *Crush It!* The lessons he took away radically changed the way he ran his business and helped it grow.

1. Embrace Your DNA: "I probably owe my marriage to this idea. Before reading the book, my wife and I were trying to do everything at once—design new products, build them, market them, find new retailers domestically and internationally, keep up with customer service, ship everything in a timely manner . . . manage employees, etc. This created a lot of friction because I really sucked at everything except designing new products, creating content, and talking to new and potential customers. After reading the book, she and I decided to outsource everything to outside contractors or hire people that brought in the qualities that I did not have."

His epiphany also helped him figure out which side of the business he should concentrate on.

"I realized that I wasn't an engineer—the books I was writing were fairly complex electrical engineering ideas that I was simplifying to bring them to an audience that wanted them, but my heart wasn't in it as much as it was with creating something new, something that inspires other artists to use it as a tool to make *their* art, and creating something with my name on it—something that my great-grandkids will be able to look back on one day and say, 'That was my great-grandpa.' So, I stopped selling all of the DIY products and focused on just that."

1. Storytell: "At the time, many of the other companies were faceless. I simply started being myself in an authentic way and became the first president of a musical instrument company who did his own product demos. This was very odd at the time to many other companies. However, our customers loved it! They realized that I was an actual guitar player who happened to make pedals, rather than an engineer who happened to dabble in a little bit of guitar. This difference, though it may seem minor, was huge for us, and a key to our success."

2. Go Deep, Not Wide: "Analytics don't tell the whole story. In a nutshell, I decided to stop chasing numbers and focus more on creating content that brought more value to our customers. A thousand views and a hundred comments are much better than ten thousand views and one comment."

3. Everyone Needs to Become a Brand: "I insisted that everyone who worked for me become a face of the company alongside me. They had to understand that everything they posted online reflected the brand. Equally important to me, by understanding the fact that everyone is basically a brand, they would have an advantage over others should they decide to pursue something else outside of my company."

4. You Got to Be You: "I jumped in with both feet, convinced that, if I followed my passion with extreme vigor, something, somewhere would happen. . . . I just had to be patient and work harder than anyone else in my niche."

Patience

It's interesting that passion and patience go hand in hand. To live in line with your passion will probably require that you go slower than you might want to. It will definitely mean that you say no more than you say yes. Bide your time; you cheapen yourself when you make deals while holding your nose. Remember, you're only crushing it if you're living entirely on your own terms.

It's not impossible to make bank when you build a business with the sole goal of getting rich, but very often entrepreneurs who get rich quickly sacrifice their chances for wealth for the long term. When I was just starting to grow my family business, my friends who graduated college at the same time that I did also went to work. They started making money and spending it on trips to Vegas and hot girls and nice watches. Me? I was making money, too. In the first five or six years, I grew that business to $45 million, and not many years later, it was a $60 million wine empire. When a normal twenty-six-year-old dude builds a $60 million business, he leverages it for twenty-year-old dude things. Yet I lived in a one-bedroom apartment in Springfield, New Jersey. I drove a Jeep Grand Cherokee. I had no watches, no suits, and no flash. I could have paid myself hundreds of thousands of dollars per year, but the most I took was $60K. I kept my head down like an ox with a plow, putting almost every dime I earned back into the business and focusing all my energy on building a personal brand around unparalleled customer service, both in the store and online. When not talking to customers, I was the most boring human being on the planet. Today I not only have everything I ever wanted (except the Jets), like all the other entrepreneurs in this book, but also I'm having the time of my life. Some achieved success in a relatively short time; most worked their asses off for years before anyone knew who they were.

You have no reason to start acting like something special until you actually have something special to show for it. Even then, don't act special; the moment you do, you'll start moving in the opposite direction. Take my advice: eat shit for as long as you have to. That means be a bigger man or woman than everyone around you. That means the customer is always right. That means you put your employees ahead of you. That means you don't take many vacations, maybe for years, and your only time off is to mark important holidays and to be there for your family (or your friends who are like family). Be patient. Be methodical. Pay off your debts. Unless your brand is glamorous, live simply, and even then be practical and calculated. Put yourself last. Once you've reached your brand and business goals, *then* you can start living it up (without putting yourself into debt, because that's insane).

HOW I'M CRUSHING IT

Alex "Nemo" Hanse, Foolies Limited Clothing Company

IG: @FOOLIES

The day after Alex "Nemo" Hanse turned thirty, he was in New Orleans to try to meet a few women.

Not just any women. Specifically, some of the stars listed on his T-shirt, like Taraji P. Henson and Ava DuVernay, who were in town to attend the Essence Festival, a four-day megacelebration of black culture in general and black women in particular. It's the T-shirt that put his clothing brand, Foolies Limited Clothing Company, on the map.

But what's really interesting about his presence at the gathering is how he got there.

His fans and customers gave him birthday money to pay for it. They literally sent him the money to buy himself a plane ticket so he could attend and connect with people who could help him grow his brand.

That's some pretty spectacular customer love and loyalty. Alex must have been doing something right.

Alex has always had a strong entrepreneurial spirit. His mother died when he was in the fifth grade, and since he didn't have a father figure, he was taken in by a family friend (who had twelve kids of her own). He was grateful to have a roof, but at school he got tired of getting picked on for his raggedy clothes and shoes, so he'd carry around a big duffel bag stuffed with chips, candy bars, and Capri Suns that he could sell to earn a little money. He also worked after school at a car wash, where he got paid under the table because he was underage. "I was just trying to survive."

In 2005, when he was a student at the University of Florida, Alex was a rapper. "Dropping bars and spitting hot lines of fire . . . at least, in my mind I was." While Googling "How to create a brand for a rapper," he found an article that said a rapper needed to create an identity for his fans. So he and his "brother of another color," Billy, a big supporter of his music, worked to come up with some kind of catchphrase. "And we're sitting around saying, 'Man, this idea sounds so foolish. This is so foolish of us.' We kept repeating it and playing around, and we started saying, 'Yeah, we're Foolies.' And it was like, 'What's a Foolie?' And I said, 'I guess somebody who's dumb enough to try something and figure it out in the end.'"

After graduating in 2009 with a degree in sports medicine, Alex couldn't find a job, so he kept concentrating on his music while working at an AT&T store. Then he and Billy decided that rappers needed a clothing line. They had no money, so they ironed the word FOOLIES on a dirty white

T-shirt. They did what Alex calls the Daymond John effect: "Put it on one person, take a picture, you take it off. Put it on another person, take a picture, take it off. Because you don't have money so you can't give shirts to everyone, but if you can post pictures on Facebook and Twitter and make it seem like everyone has a shirt, maybe other people will want it, too. And that's what started happening for us, slowly."

The shirts were created to bring attention to Alex's music, but they soon became his main output. He came up with clever ways to deliver an extra special experience to his customers. When he had a special sale, he'd send customers who bought a shirt a custom link to a YouTube video of himself singing a song with their name in it, or some other personal message. He shipped the shirts inside miniature paint cans, the idea being that when you opened the can you'd be releasing your dreams. And he'd send a handwritten letter to every customer, along with a dream journal, "because that's the biggest thing that people don't do: they don't write their goals down, so they can never manifest and come to life."

As soon as customers received their order, they'd post a picture to social media. Except, interestingly, sometimes they didn't post the shirt—they posted the letter, the can, or the dream journal. They'd thank Alex, saying it had been years since anyone had written them a letter, and some attached the letters to their refrigerators or bathroom walls.

The company eked out an existence, barely, while Alex kept working a day job, tutored, mentored at Boys and Girls Clubs, and couch-surfed. It was hard going, but he kept at it. Reading *Crush It!* in 2015 "was a confirmation that I wasn't crazy. I'd go to pitch competitions and these fake investors would chew me out: 'How is that scalable? Why are you writing letters to every customer?' I started reading the book and thought, *Man, somebody finally gets me.* It was like finding a long-lost friend or meeting your twin after being separated and you didn't even know you had one."

He realized his problem was that he wasn't creating enough content. "I went all-out motivational, plastering Facebook with posts."

In September 2015, he watched on television as Viola Davis won her first Emmy. That same night, Regina King won her first Emmy, too. "I was bawling. My brand has never deliberately focused on black women, but they've always supported me. So I was like, 'Man, we need to make something motivational based off of this dopeness that these black girls are doing.' That's when we listed all the phrases, like a regular graphic."

The graphic was a list of ways in which people could emulate the black female powerhouses of our era: WRITE LIKE SHONDA. SPEAK LIKE VIOLA. WALK LIKE KERRY [WASHINGTON]. BE FIERCE LIKE TARAJI. BE STRONG LIKE REGINA. LEAD LIKE AVA.

"I posted the graphic right before work at about eight thirty in the morning, and around maybe ten fifteen, my phone started buzzing. So I go to my Facebook page and I see forty-plus shares. I had gotten shares before, but this was a weird number, and it kept increasing. What was going on?"

The reason Alex's phone was buzzing incessantly was because best-selling author, speaker, and digital strategist Luvvie Ajayi, aka Awesomely Luvvie, had posted the graphic to her page. She messaged him and told him he needed to put those names on a shirt. "She didn't even know I had a T-shirt company. She just thought I was a random guy, which is crazy how God works and how everything just lines up."

Then Ava DuVernay reposted the graphic on Twitter.

"It started freaking going everywhere." Alex quickly added a few more names to the graphic—LUPITA [NYONG'O], UZO [ADUBA], ANGELA [BASSETT], and QUEEN [LATIFAH]—and turned it into a T-shirt with the Foolies logo on the back.

That detail, the logo placement, is important to what happened next.

A few months later, on a Wednesday, Alex got an e-mail from *Essence* asking for shirts for a youth choir to use at an event called Black Women in Hollywood. They needed them by Sunday in time to tape the show later in the week.

"It was a Hail Mary mission." It usually took weeks to get T-shirts printed, and on top of that, he had just switched printing companies because the previous one kept blowing him off. The new company managed to give him a quick turnaround time, and he shipped the shirts in time for the event.

There was no footage when the event itself happened, but soon afterward he got an Instagram alert. It was a picture of the girls wearing his T-shirt, and standing there with her arms around them was Oprah Winfrey.

He'd had no idea the event was sponsored by the Oprah Winfrey Network (OWN).

He and his COO, Kim, started plastering the shirt everywhere they could. When the show aired on OWN, at first there was no sign of the choir. Alex was sure the segment had been cut. Then, right after a commercial break, there they were.

The T-shirts looked fantastic, but Alex realized that maybe putting the logo on the back instead of the front hadn't been such a good idea. "We had wanted the shirt to be about the graphic, not about us, and we wanted to make sure that our customers knew that we always had their backs. Real smart, genius."

That night Shonda Rhimes tweeted out a picture of the shirt, tagged to Foolies, and posted it to Instagram, too. "I've never gotten so many notifications in my life," says Alex.

Since then, any money Alex has earned has gone back into the business or into free shirts for influencers. There are a few new versions of the shirt, listing different actors. He tries to attend as many conferences as he can where he will meet other influencers, volunteering to work there because he usually can't afford the ticket price. He recently received a comped ticket to the BlogHer conference from someone who heard him speak about Foolies at another event several months earlier and wanted to make sure he could go.

He's committed to motivating people to reach their goals with more than just a T-shirt. "I don't want to just sell you T-shirts. What happens if you don't buy one? Is it now over for you to be motivated? Why not serve just to serve?" To that end, he launched a podcast called Dream Without Limits Radio, where he collects stories of dreamers, game changers, and people living out their purpose.

So the podcast numbers are interesting. I think more people are following me as a whole than necessarily listening to the podcast. The episodes will fluctuate, so we'll probably see two or three hundred, or we'll see fifty, forty-five. I'm OK with those numbers only because the responses that I get and the people, they're the fifty or two hundred who really want it. It doesn't sound as cool because I don't have tens of thousands of listeners, but I know those fifty or two hundred are the ones who are actually taking it and doing something with it, and that's what I'd rather have. Because they're gonna be the ones who give me two, three, four thousand later.

I get to bring on people of color and women, who don't get highlighted enough. You'll see all these dope women on there. I love guys, but I know where my market is, and my niche. People tell me, "Oh, you need to expand and talk to all these people," and I'm like, "Gary gets it."

Alex mentored a lot of students at the University of Florida and continues to visit middle and high schools to talk to them about entrepreneurship and getting out of the 'hood. When his brand started to take off, a number of his former mentees told him that it made perfect sense that this would be his calling. "This has always been what you've been doing. Now it's just in the form of a clothing company."

Speed

I love a good contradiction, but this isn't one. Patience is for the long term; speed is for the short term. The pressure that builds between the two produces the diamond.

Speed is one of my two or three obsessions in business. I will always gravitate toward the thing that allows me to live my life more efficiently and do my work faster. It's one of the reasons I'm so excited about voice-controlled assistants like Google Home and Amazon Echo (see more on page 245). Entrepreneurs—heck, humans!—care about time and convenience, and it's just faster to spit the toothpaste out and say, "OK, Google, remind me to buy more toothpaste," than it is to grab your phone and type "toothpaste" into your shopping list. If you're just starting out, you're going to be slogging it alone for a long time before you can hire an assistant to help you manage your time. In the meantime, put whatever tools you can find to good use to keep you moving through the day and using your time wisely and efficiently.

You need to constantly be in do mode. I see you out there over-thinking your content and agonizing over your decisions, taking forever to make up your mind. Your confidence is low, and you're worried people will call you a loser if you make the wrong call. Get over that quick. I love losing because I learn so much from it. The reason I don't talk about my failures much is not because I'm hiding anything, but because once I've seen I've made a mistake, in my mind, it's over. I'll admit it: I was wrong in 2010; location-based chat app Yobongo was not the next great startup. But what good does it do me to dwell on what didn't work out? I'd rather look ahead to the next thing that I'm sure will. My track record speaks for itself. Being unafraid of making mistakes makes everything easy for me. Not worrying about what people think frees you to do things, and doing things allows you to win or learn from your loss—which means you win either way. Hear me now: you are better off being wrong ten times and being right three than you are if you try only three times and always get it right.

HOW I'M CRUSHING IT

Timothy Roman, Imperial Kitchen & Bath

IG: @IMPERIALKB

Timothy Roman got by with a little help from his friends.

Once he got rid of the old ones, that is.

Timothy is the son of Russian immigrants who brought him to the United States nineteen years ago, when he was eleven. His parents got busy doing what immigrants do: working, trying to get by, and adjusting to a new country, a new language, and a new way of life. They expected Timothy to do his part by doing well in school and getting into college.

Problem was, Timothy hated school. "I failed everything miserably. I couldn't concentrate. Always, my head was floating around. I was always doodling some stuff, whether it was plans, or ideas, or dreams, or counting my profits. I don't recall any formal education."

The profits Timothy is referring to were from his dual revenue stream. See, he was putting his natural entrepreneurial tendencies to use. By the time he started high school, he was DJ-ing and selling mixes. He was also selling weed. In tenth grade, when he realized he was making the same amount of money as his teachers, he told his mother he was dropping out and getting his GED. She thought he was dropping out to be a DJ, and that was indeed the original plan; the drug dealing was just supposed to be supplemental income. Pretty soon, though, things reversed, and for about ten years, that was Timothy's life.

"I was in a poor neighborhood. Nobody has the knowledge or anything to influence you enough to say, 'Hey, you know, you can maybe try to do something legally, and try to become an entrepreneur, and start a small business, and work really hard, and try doing that.' You know, that wasn't even a conversation."

Until he finally wound up in jail (which is how his mother found out how her son was really making his living).

When he got out a month later, he was determined to change. He started by eliminating all his old friends and making new ones.

"One was doing Web development and SEO [search-engine optimization]. Another was selling high-end real estate. Another one was selling high-end furniture. But all created these situations themselves and were like-minded. We really clicked immediately. They respected me, and I couldn't wait to learn the way it's supposed to be done."

The friend who sold real estate let Timothy crash on his couch. He also introduced Timothy to his father, who owned a construction company, who then offered Timothy a position. At the same time, Timothy, who thought he might like to be a website designer, was spending a lot of time trying to educate himself via YouTube. That's how he somehow came across a Gary Vee video. "I find out that he's Russian and that his parents are immigrants, and immediately there's this crazy connection and I really get sucked in. I got hooked." He plowed through all the video material he could find, and when he realized the only other way to get more information was through *Crush It!*, he read that, too, even though reading was so difficult for him that he'd read only one book (Tony Hsieh's *Delivering Happiness*) in his life until that point.

I'd never had a sounding board, no one to say, "Hey, you know, you can do this. Go out there; get it done." The message from *Crush It!* was, no matter where you are, who you are, color of your skin, where you're from, size, shape, and all that good stuff, if you really feel like you're good at something, if you put in the work, I guarantee you, you will get somewhere. You know, it's hard to get your mind around it when you have no experience with that, but I kinda just took it and ran with it.

That was the end of 2012. Within six to eight months of working with his friend's father, Timothy was sure that he wanted to start his own company, a kitchen and bath specialty contractor. In two-and-a-half years, he went from pushing paper to closing projects, becoming the owner's right-hand man. That was just during the day. After work, until two or three a.m., Timothy studied.

I would learn everything I possibly could about the construction industry, read magazines, learn architects' names. I wanted to have so much information on day one of my business that if I had a conversation with a client, I could deliver so much value. I was trying to learn so much about the product that people would not look at my age and lack of experience as a weak point but overlook that when I told them everything that I know.

I was computer savvy and had some basic skills, so I would work on the website. I would try to write content. Contractors didn't have proper marketing materials. Forget about SEO. The ones who had websites were really big companies with ten trucks. Your regular kitchen-and-bath guys were all in their forties, fifties, and sixties and have been in business for twenty or thirty years. They've established so many relationships that some are doing business literally through word of mouth. I knew that it would take me years to establish word of mouth the traditional way. I was doing things that other contractors didn't even understand, and it was very time-consuming. We didn't have all the apps that we have today that can automate it for you.

Through his work, he'd developed relationships with subcontractors, and with his boss's blessing, he spent all his time outside of his day job planting the seeds for his own company through Facebook and YouTube. Little by little, people started to engage with his content. If someone liked a picture, Timothy sent a thank-you message. If someone e-mailed for an estimate and he was able to get an address, that person got a thank-you note and small gifts around the holidays. He landed his first projects by the middle of 2015. Fortunately, he didn't have to be at work until 9:30 a.m., which gave him several hours to focus on his own projects before his day had even officially started. This meant that by lunchtime, he could just run out to check on his subcontractors' work, leaving his evenings free for e-mails and sales work.

Once he had three projects lined up, he informed his boss he was ready to quit. His schedule didn't ease up, though. He just filled those hours with more work, more engagement, and more content creation. He uses Snapchat Stories and Instagram Stories to share behind-the-scenes peeks at projects, and now that he has a showroom, he can easily introduce new products when they come in.

Two years after going out on his own, Timothy's company crossed the million-dollar sales mark, with projections to hit $2.5M to 3.0M by the end of 2017.

"You know, I make sacrifices and crazy decisions every day, knowing that it's all going to work out. Now it just becomes routine. Owning your own business sounds really, really scary, and it's a lot of responsibility. But Gary was like, 'What's the worst that could happen? Go for it. The market will tell you if you've got it or not.'"

Incidentally, Timothy's mother is incredibly proud. "My mother is in tears every time I tell her about some new accomplishment, or project that I've done, or a milestone I've crossed. It's just been, you know, really great."

Work

I've audited a lot of people over the years who on the surface seemed to be doing everything right. They'd established a good niche, they were personable and interesting, their content was on target and valuable, yet they expressed frustration that they weren't meeting their business goals. When I looked closer, I'd see that they were still playing golf or tweeting about the previous night's *Walking Dead* episode. Let me make this as clear as I can:

When you first start out, there is no time for leisure—if you want to crush it. There is no time for YouTube videos or shooting the shit in the breakroom or an hour-and-a-half lunch. That is, of course, why entrepreneurship is often seen as a young person's game. It takes a lot of stamina to get a personal brand and business off the ground. It *is* a lot easier to devote all your time to a new business endeavor when you're twenty-five and single with no one to answer to but yourself. Still, 95 percent of the people reading this book, even the young ones, probably have some kind of obligation: college loans (many are likely still in school), mortgages, child support, elderly parents, or dependent families. Most probably already have a job. Maybe you've got a flexible schedule because you're driving for a rideshare company or working part-time or nights. But most of you are working nine to five or even eight to six. Your only prayer to one day live the *Crush It!* life, there-fore, is to deploy ungodly amounts of work from seven p.m. to two a.m. Monday through Friday, plus all day Saturdays and Sundays. Ideally you'll be building your business around the thing you love to do for fun and relaxation, so it won't feel like losing your leisure time. The only additional thing you will have time for is your family. They de-serve to get the best of you, so make sure you don't let the work creep in to all of your time with them—unless you can make them part of it, which would be wonderful. Bring them in on this adventure with you! Many people interviewed for this book have done this. Rodrigo Tasca hired his sister to help him build his video production business, and they worked out of his bedroom in their parents' house. Jared Polin and Lauryn Evarts both regularly featured their grandmothers on their blogs. Rich Roll's children and his wife, Julie, are a constant presence in his videos and photographs, and the couple are listed as coauthors on their first cookbook. When Brittany Xavier books a mother-daughter Mother's Day branding opportunity or photo shoot, she puts a portion of the fee in an account set aside for her daughter, because without her child, these opportunities wouldn't exist. Since she turned nine, Chad Collins's daughter Jordyn has run the trivia events conducted at Brick Fest Live, the nationwide LEGO event that grew out of the LEGO YouTube channel they built together. This is what the modern-day family business can look like.*

You have to decide how you're going to spend your time. Start by blocking off the hours you must spend on your obligations—your job, your kids, your spouse, your aging mother. If you're serious about crushing it, every minute not spent on those obligations should be spent producing content, distributing content, engaging with your community, or engaging in business development. Stephen Marinaro

---

* As much as I share about my daily life, my wife and children are off-limits. We'll revisit the issue later when the children are older and can decide for themselves if they want to have a public presence connected to my brand. It's a decision Lizzie and I made for our family, but I wholly support anyone who makes a different choice.

(IG: @TheSalonGuy), who was a hairstylist, a DJ, a fireman, and a fugitive recovery agent before becoming YouTube's TheSalonGuy, one of the largest professional hair channels on the platform, was relentless in his quest to build his brand. "If you sit on your butt all day waiting for things to come to you, nothing is going to happen." Once just a vlogger who might film himself demonstrating haircutting techniques, his dogged persistence led him to being featured on reality-TV episodes, making appearances on *Good Morning America* and Fox News, covering the Oscars, and becoming a fixture at New York Fashion Week events, where he interviewed celebrities and designers. He went from earning a total of $20K four years ago to being able to charge thousands of dollars per month to offer media services to brands.

Do things! Create content daily. Biz-dev daily. Meet with two or three people per day who can get you awareness, distribution, or sales—somehow closer to your goals. DM people on Instagram with offers to collaborate (instructions on page 225). You should be taking these actions twelve, fifteen hours per day. If you're working another job, you should be cramming as much work as you can in the three or four hours you have to yourself per night (or day, if you work the night shift). And don't forget to sleep. Six to eight hours of sleep per day or night is ideal for most people. Just make every minute of your remaining sixteen to eighteen hours count.

Do you think this kind of relentless work ethic sounds unhealthy? Does it sound like too much? Pay attention to those feelings. Self-awareness is vitally important.

Crushing it is about living on your own terms, equally satisfied with your income and your life. You will get no judgment from me if your goals are modest. I have obnoxious ambition, but I don't think everyone else should, and I don't want anyone to think I've got a mold and expect everyone who reads this to force themselves to fit into it. But please, if you're not willing to do the grind, for God's sake do not complain when your business doesn't grow as fast or as big as you want it to. Maybe you decide to spend two hours a week volunteering at the animal shelter or the food bank, or maybe you decide to join a cycling club. You go to the movies. You play mobile games during your flights. That's fine! It probably makes you a better person. But then accept that your ambitions are humbler than you originally thought and be good with it. Not everyone should try to build a business as big as it can get. The truth is that you can't do it all, so you're going to have to make choices. Be practical. Raising your self-awareness and suffocating any self-delusion is a crucial piece of keeping you on the path to success, however you define it.

Crushing it follows the laws of thermodynamics: whatever energy you put into something will manifest itself in equal amounts when it comes out. Sometimes that resulting energy gets harnessed to move muscles or machines; sometimes it dissipates, unused, into the ether. A successful entrepreneur is one who puts in enough energy to move the gears and executes well enough so the work isn't wasted.

HOW I'M CRUSHING IT

Deon Graham, Digital Architect

IG: @DEON

Deon Graham was a tennis pro. Now he's Diddy's digital director.

He's only thirty-one, but already he has one of the most coveted jobs in the marketing world.

That's what personal branding can do for a person.

This story starts in 2008, in Miami. During the day, Deon was teaching tennis. At night, he was spending too much money at the clubs and "doing young people stuff."

He noticed there was a void in the marketplace. Clubs wanted to market only to a certain type—white, Hispanic, etc.—and while they liked having hip-hop parties because the revenue was good, they shied away from projecting the image of having a heavy hip-hop crowd. No marketing company was focusing on clubs that catered to an urban or hip-hop audience. So Deon decided he would.

He created the nightlife website City Never Sleeps. By offering to market the club brands on his site, he circumvented the owners' reluctance to prominently market their hip-hop nights. Partygoers got access to their photos, and club owners got access to patrons. People loved the site, so he knew he was on to something, but there was no money in it.

But Deon says that was kind of his fault. "I was just trying to make deals and make moves for a profit. I wasn't trying to build a brand. I wasn't committed to the branding process; I was committed to try to make money."

It wasn't until he started to dive into *Crush It!* principles and focus on building a brand for the long term that things started to turn around. He started being more selective about the caliber of clubs he worked with, turning down money if he didn't think the club was on brand and would lead to bigger clients. "All my decision making changed. The reactions I was getting from people changed, and not coincidentally, the checks started to get bigger."

He'd been engaging people on Twitter and Facebook, but not as much as he should have been. He started watching Gary Vee. "This guy has all these followers, he looks like he has a more successful business than me, but every day he's on social media talking to people, giving them advice, giving them free content. So why am I not doing that?"

He doubled down on the engagement. "It was 24/7. Literally anybody mentioning anything, I would join conversations, reply to everybody. If it was two a.m. and there was a popping party going on, we were in those conversations, letting people know about other parties in the city. There was no room for anything else." After landing a contract with a prominent nightlife group, he felt secure enough to quit his day job.

The site's popularity rose quickly until his was the biggest platform catering to the urban and hip-hop market. He was approached by Cîroc vodka's marketing team, Blue Flame Agency.

"They asked, 'Did you make this site?'"

"Yeah."

"We've paid people $75,000 to build a website."

"I said, 'I'll do it for $10,000.' I just wanted to get in the building."

And he did. Blue Flame Agency hired him, and from then on he was busy with project after project. For two-and-a-half years, he brokered deals with Hennessy, LVMH (Louis Vuitton Moët Hennessy), any brand you could think of that would want to reach the urban nightlife consumer.

In 2015, Aubrey Flynn of Combs Enterprises offered Deon a position as his digital director, working with eight different brands, including a tequila, a TV network, and a music label.

It's a busy life. Deon has a family, so a lot of the work is done after his three kids are asleep and before everyone wakes up. His in-box has been flooded with requests for speaking engagements since his mention in the May 2017 issue of *Entrepreneur* magazine.

He's got massive ambition, and nothing is going to get in his way.

> I'm definitely going to have a digital agency similar to what Gary's running, doing what I do for Sean Combs with many different brands and celebrities.
>
> Sometimes I go to these meetings, and you kind of get a different look, just based on being a young black male. That's actually been the hardest part, getting taken seriously by the corporate world. That's why it's good to be aligned with someone like Sean Combs, who fights for that. But it's definitely a different conversation when I go into these rooms, than for say, Gary. I walk in the door and they definitely get surprised. You can tell they were thinking or looking for someone else. It's just something I gotta deal with; can't use it as an excuse.
>
> The most important thing is to be fully committed and to block out any noise, because nobody has done what you're attempting to do. And the only way to get it is to put the blinders on and push forward.

Attention

Where are the eyeballs going? What are your customers talking about? What are the newest trends in your field? What are the biggest controversies? You have to pay attention to everything. One of my great advantages has been the ability to see where the attention is shifting even as my competition is looking elsewhere (usually backward).

Knowing how to spot underpriced or underappreciated attention is a key influencer skill. People have always dismissed or underestimated the new thing, from radio to TV, from the Internet to the social networks. They're the same people who believe that Hollywood, not YouTube and Instagram, still incubates the biggest stars. As anyone under the age of twenty-five will tell you, they're wrong.

Don't become so comfortable on one platform that you don't take the time to develop solid skills on the others. On the other hand, don't cling to your favorite even when it's become ineffective or overpriced. Keep experimenting even when you're sure you're doing it right. Your willingness to risk discomfort will save you in the long run. There are a lot of you whose competitors were mastering Instagram five years ago just in case it got really big, while you were still debating whether to get an account. Don't make that mistake again.

HOW I'M CRUSHING IT

Andrew Nguyen, Brand with Drew

IG:@BRANDWITHDREW

"My market started on Facebook, then jumped onto Twitter. They got away from Facebook, then jumped onto Instagram. They got away from Twitter, then jumped back into Facebook. And Snapchat, too." Where the attention goes, so goes Andrew Nguyen.

Andrew may follow the eyeballs, but he has always marched to his own beat. At seventeen, he tried to follow a traditional path and please his immigrant parents by accepting a scholarship to a small school in Hampton, Virginia, with the intention of studying to become a pharmacist. By the end of the first semester, he was failing almost every class. Thinking it might suit him better, he switched over to a five-year MBA program.

He didn't tell his parents.

It was summer before he finally confessed. Naturally, they were livid. They also pointed out that if he was just going to get an MBA, he could go to school in their home state of Maryland and get his degree for a lot less money. But Andrew wasn't willing to leave Hampton, because he had already started making a name for himself there—first as a barber. Andrew had learned to cut his own hair from his father, who had attended barber school after arriving in the United States from Vietnam. When Andrew realized he was in a dorm full of men who needed haircuts, he saw opportunity and hung a barber sign outside his door. Business was good; sometimes he cut ten or more heads per day. He was also gaining a reputation as a DJ. He'd noticed that the most popular DJ on campus was a senior. Someone was going to have to take his place when he graduated. He thought, *Why not me?* He used his barber money to buy a set of speakers and some DJ equipment and had them sent to the dorm. He started out doing a few events for free, again building his brand, until the reigning DJ noticed his potential and took him under his wing, making the necessary introductions to get Andrew good paying clients. "I truly felt this was something I was meant to do. I was meant to stay at this school, meant to meet the people that I was to meet, meant to grow these businesses. I got to the point where, once I realized that I truly believed in this vision, I was willing to do whatever it took to do it."

Andrew's mother and father were not pleased and essentially disowned him. He was on his own, without even enough money to pay for lodging. He wound up living in his car and working in the school cafeteria so he'd have access to food. He became a reservist in the US Marine Corps to help pay his tuition. Eventually, however, he built his DJ brand into a thriving six-figure business serving the campus and the city (his predecessor-turned-mentor, Taylor Austin James, would become better known as DJ Tay James, Justin Bieber's official DJ).

Andrew didn't have to cut hair anymore, but he was marked by the months of homelessness. Saving money became his priority. He decided to use his MBA to get a job that would allow him to build up a financial foundation as well as teach him the logistics of the corporate world. He took a sales and marketing job with Pepsi. At the same time, he decided to start his own marketing agency, the O Agency.

"My passion wasn't barbering or DJ-ing. My passion was branding myself to become this DJ, this facade, this brand. There's a psychological quality to branding and marketing that's sometimes hard to quantify. You have to care and show people the quality of who you are and what you do."

To test his knowledge and skills, he also decided to develop a marketing plan for his friend Bakari Taylor, a trainer who had earned some local notoriety for his brand, Body by Bakari, through a series of free boot camps he had held around the DC area the summer before. Taylor had the skills and charisma, Andrew had the business and marketing background. Together, they launched a big branding initiative, an East Coast No Excuses tour to help build brand awareness.

The tour was a huge success, but it almost broke Andrew. "That was the hardest year of my life, even past sleeping in my car and going into the Marine Corps. I knew that most businesses fail, I knew that the odds were against me, and I knew that I was not supposed to make it, so I was waking up at four or five in the morning to work twelve-hour days for Pepsi, then working six p.m. to two a.m., putting in time for the O Agency and Bakari. And I was still DJ-ing, too."

Thank God Pepsi made energy drinks, which Andrew could get for free.

Within one year, he was done. He quit the DJ business and put in his two-weeks' notice at Pepsi. Within six months of launching the O Agency, he'd acquired his first NFL client. Today he works with brands like 7-Eleven and Sotheby's.

He read *Crush It!* only about two years ago, but it was reaffirming. "Hearing someone who's many, many levels ahead of me saying things that I've already thought . . . the overall mentality is what really excites me. There was so much confirmation that I was doing the right thing."

Until recently, he always prioritized the O Agency brand, preferring to wait until he had something to show for his efforts before putting his personal brand forward.

"You can brand yourself all you want, but if you don't have credibility or have not done anything, it's almost worthless. You can only sell something that's actually good."

Now that he has been able to "liberate" himself from the business, he has started building his personal brand, @BrandwithDrew.

I'm at a point right now where I realize I will probably never be broke again in my life. I've truly found my passion. And one of the things I truly want to do is help out a lot of people who are lost, especially the millennial market. I would go even deeper by saying the minority market. That's the niche that I'm really going after and putting myself in a position where I can really help people out. It's not about the money. I do a lot of things for free because I care more about impact than the monetary things.

I don't even consider what I'm doing as work anymore. I enjoy what I do so much. I want to continue speaking and building my own brand and writing books and creating events that help people. I would love to do that for the rest of my life.

These are the first seven essentials to a strong personal brand. I hope they sound familiar to readers of the original *Crush It!* It would be impossible to say these things too much or too often. You know how I know? Because for the number of times I repeat myself every year, there should be thousands and thousands more of you reaching your goals. The only explanation that such a large percentage of you aren't is that you're not taking me at my word. I exaggerate a lot for emphasis and entertainment, but I am not kidding when I tell you that if you scrimp in any way on any one of these building blocks, you will falter. It's just the truth.

There's an eighth essential. It's the only one that has seen some significant developments over the years. It's so important, it deserves a chapter of its own.

THE EIGHTH ESSENTIAL—CONTENT

To monetize your personal brand into a business using social marketing networks, two pillars need to be in place: product and content.

—*Crush It!*, chapter 5

It's still true that the right product and content will be key to building a vibrant personal brand. That part never changes. But how you develop your content and increase its reach definitely has. In *Crush It!* I recommended simultaneously pumping out content onto all the different channels using a social-media Web service (anyone remember Ping.fm?). It was only later, however, that I realized there had been another misunderstanding. I should have specified that I didn't mean you should pump out the *same* content across multiple platforms. Rather, I wanted you to develop high-quality native microcontent. For those of you new to this, that means content that is specifically and perfectly designed to suit the platform you're using to disseminate it. The audience on Twitter isn't looking for the same kind of content as Instagram followers. A Facebook post will have greater impact if it's not just a cut-and-paste job from your blog or a ten-minute video that should actually be living on YouTube. Even if your audience overlaps among the platforms, people are in a completely different mindset when they're visiting one platform than when visiting another. If they're on Twitter, they're likely trying to keep up with current news. If they're on Facebook, they're probably catching up with friends and family. They may go to Snapchat to consume a blip of entertainment on their lunch break, but they'll go to YouTube when they're in the mood to settle in for the evening with some long-form video, the same way previous generations watched TV. You should be plotting how to adapt your content to appeal to every platform your audience might visit in a given day.

Creating all that content can seem daunting, but it's a lot more manageable if you focus on creating one big piece of pillar content that can be splintered into other smaller bits of content—content that breeds like rabbits, if you will. The concept can best be illustrated by a chart my team and I created for VaynerTalent, a division of Vayner-Media I established for influencers who have grown their personal brands as big as they can on their own and need extra help to keep growing. It's a service for the 1 percent of the 1 percent. If you're reading this book, you're likely not there yet, but I hope to teach you what you need to know so that if you get good enough, you'll need us one day. Anyway, we use a chart to illustrate our strategy for creating endless bits of microcontent out of one "pillar" piece of content:

What those pieces of content actually look like, and the platforms you choose to use, is what you're here to figure out. More on that in part II.

In *Crush It!* I also established that great content is a result of passion plus expertise. While the opportunities for people to become stars on various social-media platforms have multiplied, to have a prayer of becoming even the eighty-eighth best whiskey Instagrammer, you're going to have to make sure that you are constantly updating your knowledge and providing information and insight that people can't find easily anywhere else. Moreover, you'll have to do it in a unique and memorable signature style. There's no way around it—your content must be amazing. For some that reality can be as paralyzing as a snakebite. Here's the antivenin: you don't have to wait until you're an expert or you've designed a perfect website or written ten perfect blog posts before launching a business. Quite the contrary.

Document, Don't Create

In 2009, I devoted only three lines to the idea that "you can even make the learning process part of your content." It was an aside, a possible solution if you were young or still building cred. Since then I've come to realize that, actually, the learning process should be your content. That means it's not a problem if you've got more passion than expertise. Our best-loved icons aren't the ones born to the manor who stayed in the manor. They're the ones who started out tinkering in their basements, who sold product out of the backs of their cars, who rose and fell and rose again. The only ones we can't forgive are people who won't admit to their imperfections or own their mistakes.

It's true that great content hinges on great storytelling and that every story in the universe has already been told. But not by you. You are unique, and you provide nuance, perspective, and details that no one else can. That means you don't just have the ability to generate unique pieces of creative—you *are* the unique piece of creative. Don't worry about getting people's attention by plotting a poetic YouTube video or writing four drafts of a snappy Facebook status post. Instead, use every platform available to document your actual life and speak your truth. Let people learn who you are, then let them watch you develop into who you want to become.

At the end of 2015, DRock, my videographer, started following me around with a video camera everywhere I went during work hours. The only time the camera was turned off was during sensitive meetings or when I went to the bathroom. I wanted people to see what hustle really looked like, how I could squeeze so much productivity into every minute (and incidentally, to prove that even when you've "made it" and are "important," you don't have to act like an arrogant jerk to the people you interact with on a day-to-day basis, especially those working in service jobs). It was important to me to address a frequent speculation I was seeing in my feeds, which was that I was exaggerating how many hours I worked per day. I wanted people to see that when I said I worked from about six a.m. to ten p.m. Monday through Friday, I was serious. Moreover, I have been working those hours for about a decade.

Most important, however, I wanted to provide a learning tool for the kind of people built like me. I learn by watching and doing, not by reading. It's not uncommon for me to get a message from someone who tells me that they picked up something valuable from watching me interact with people on-screen or from a random rant that I offered from the back of the car. In most cases, I'm almost positive that that moment meant nothing to anyone else, but to hear that on that day I was able to help one person means the world to me. I can't take a meeting with every person who wants my advice, but I can teach by example and let them learn from that. None of us can predict with utmost certainty exactly what's going to happen to us. We will probably meet the people we arrange to meet, but we could also have random encounters. We will probably have the conversations we have scheduled, but who knows where those talks might go? Documenting guarantees that every encounter and every engagement is captured so I can ensure that I'm never caught off guard when I experience a moment that could spark a valuable piece of content for my followers. Documenting has liberated me from the pressure of having to create all the time.

Use Snapchat, Instagram Stories, YouTube videos, and Facebook Live three, four, five times per day to share the world through your eyes. Let your audience meet your cranky uncle, let them see what you're eating for lunch, let them follow you as you slog through the workout you love to hate. Invite them in when you move into your first postdivorce apartment or your college dorm. Take them along on your vacations and business trips. Think of yourself as the star of this show *and* the production company.

Is everything about your daily life inherently interesting and new? In the right hands, yes. It's not easy to make a personal documentary, but it's a hell of a lot easier than trying to produce *Modern Family*. And which do you think you'll get done faster? What's the cost? It's worth a try. Maybe you'll hate it (it took me several months to get used to having a camera follow me wherever I went), and maybe you'll fail. But maybe you'll build the audience that earns you $80K a year, or $380K, which can come through the ads, affiliates, speaking engagements, books, sponsorship deals, and other ancillary revenue-earning opportunities that come from having a strong personal brand. You never know what you're going to put out that inspires someone important to reach out to you. People who see your work will come to you with ideas and offers and partnerships. They will buy into you if you give them the right story. At the very least, even if you don't become the next Kardashian, you'll likely find that you can healthily supplement your current income doing something that you find interesting and fun.

Documenting to build a personal brand is an especially good tactic if you're already working a job that you want to leave someday. Build your brand and gain traction in your niche before you ever need to make any money, so that when you are ready to step out of your current job, your brand is there to hold you up and carry you to your next opportunity.

Now, this tactic solves only one hurdle: how to build cred when you have none yet. However, it cannot help you if your content sucks. Sorry, there's no skirting the fact that any success you achieve will be predicated on the quality of your content. Don't think you can put out mediocre videos and blogs and get anything but mediocre results, just as you can't think that putting out a half-assed effort will get you even halfway to where you want to go. That said, just because you suck now doesn't mean you're always going to suck. Many of the entrepreneurs we spoke to didn't know what they were doing when they first started vlogging or podcasting either, and it showed. But they worked at it every day, analyzing their content, engaging with audiences to see what resonated and what didn't, and studying other personal brands to see what strategies they could adapt for themselves. They practiced their craft as intensely and methodically as a surgical resident practices her stitches or a preprofessional basketball player practices his layups.

Documenting will keep you honest. It makes me laugh when I see nineteen-year-olds and fresh college grads anoint themselves on Instagram profiles as "entrepreneur experts," or "social-media life coaches." Like hell they are. Very, very few have earned the right to those titles. Young girls will put up profiles announcing that they're beauty experts. No, they're beauty opinionators. You don't get to call yourself an expert until you've put in the work—and the market decides, not you. When I was a kid, I would sit next to my dad in the car and tell him that I was going to be a wine expert and build the biggest liquor store in the country. I couldn't drink, so I spent all the years until my twenty-first birthday tasting all the things critics and wine labels said wine tasted like—grass, dirt, cherries, tobacco—to develop my palate while I learned the business. It was only when I was of age and sure I had something of real, unique value to offer customers that I went public and started building a brand around my expertise. I was thirty years old and had been in the business of tasting hundreds of wines per week for a decade.

If I could give some advice to my seventeen-year-old self, I'd tell him to turn on the camcorder and capture every minute of his training. How fantastic would it be to be able to share with people the first time I tasted dirt? I could have filmed myself tasting thirty-five different Merlots and telling the audience, "Someday I'm going to be able to tell you which is which while blindfolded," and then three years later I could have filmed myself blind taste-testing a row of red wines and correctly identifying those Merlots. And then I could have created some content that juxtaposed those two videos and showed the world how far I had come. It would have been honest, and it would have been great storytelling. At twenty-six I was going to be who I am today; it's a shame the whole process of getting here has been lost to history. Sure, I tell my story in books and during keynotes, but imagine the detailed lessons I could have shared, the mistakes people could have watched me make, the learning curve I could have provided, if only I had thought to document my life in the moment. The beauty expert wannabes could do the same thing. Instead of going to the department store, getting makeup advice from the reps at the cosmetics counter, and then filming themselves regurgitating the information as though it were their own, they could film themselves asking questions at the makeup counter, educating their audience while educating themselves. Then they could build content with that new knowledge and refer to that video over and over.

Documenting isn't valuable because it captures how interesting (or not) you are now; it's about preparing for how people will watch you ten years from now. Cassius Clay was only twenty-one when he declared, "I am the greatest." But then he went about proving it and became Muhammad Ali. Why can't you do the same, even on a smaller level? Think about how you feel when you watch a clip of Justin Bieber singing when he was twelve, or video footage of Michael Jackson rehearsing for the *Thriller* video in a dance studio with his choreographer. Can you imagine if we could watch Vera Wang cut her first patterns and sew her first wedding dresses? Or if we could be privy to George Lucas's thoughts as he developed ideas for his student films at the University of Southern California? Not the way we can now through a biography or interviews, but captured verbatim in the moment, before they could be subject to the mental editing we all apply to our memories over time? It's an amazing thing to see talent grow and to bear witness to the evolution of greatness. Someday, you could be that kind of inspiration to others if you capture the journey.

Documenting also gives you an archive to work with that can help you validate your early promises or, as I like to call it, earn your keep. For example, people thought I was crazy in 2012 when I said that Facebook stole Instagram when it bought the company for a billion dollars. I get ridiculous pleasure releasing that old footage now that as of its last valuation, Instagram is worth $50 billion (and much more, in my opinion). Documenting your business ensures that you'll have many opportunities to say, "I told you so." I recently filmed a meeting with Kyle, a rapper *Rolling Stone* picked as one of "10 New Artists You Need to Know" in 2015. We talked music and marketing and songwriting, and it was awesome. In ten years, when he's as well known as Eminem, that video is going to be viewed thousands and thousands more times by his fans. For many, that will be their introduction to me. Even more awesome . . . for me—;).

A lot of pseudo-experts will justify subterfuge by saying they're just taking the age-old advice of fake it 'til you make it. But no one needs to do that anymore. The only reason people used to have to fake it was because they had to convince the gatekeepers—the agents, the directors, the publishers, the music producers, the talent scouts—to give them the shot they needed to prove themselves. But the Internet plays the middleman role now, and the Internet can't stop you from putting your work out there. Put your stuff up and see what the market has to say about it. Take it down if no one likes it (or keep it up for historical reference). Change it up and try again. Take risks and learn from them. Daniel Markham of the What's Inside? YouTube channel, which boasts five million subscribers, launched several video channels before he finally put up the one that got people's attention. Once it started gaining traction, he applied everything he had learned from his failures to improve his channel's content quality, user experience, and monetization strategy.

There's another reason not to fake it. The only people who fall for your act when you pretend to be something you're not are the exact same customers you're not going to want in ten years or even ten months. Simultaneously, you lose credibility with the top tier of customers you're going to need to grow and sustain your business. You're sacrificing long-term growth for short-term gains, and I think that puts entrepreneurs in a vulnerable position in the long run. Who's going to trust you when they know you're willing to snow the ignorant?

It is not OK to be manipulative; it is OK to be a novice. I hope you understand the difference. It's exciting to watch someone thoughtfully, strategically, and intelligently come into their professional own. Embrace your newness; in many ways it could give you an advantage. You will likely have a fresh energy and enthusiasm that many more-seasoned professionals have lost. That's attractive. And admitting that you're still learning will give people a reason to check in on your progress. It will also make it that much more exciting when you can finally say, "I told you so." Have you ever been watching a movie or TV show when the kid who used to star in all the school plays and talk about making it in Hollywood suddenly appears on-screen, or seen the face of someone you used to know on the cover of a national magazine? It's almost impossible not to get worked up about it. "Holy shit, I know him! He did it!" From then on, whenever the conversation makes it possible, you will probably slip in the fact that you knew that person back when nobody else did. Now, as excited as you are, imagine how excited your old acquaintance is knowing that hundreds of his old classmates are having the same reaction, especially if he was mocked or put down for daring to think he had enough talent or smarts to be a star. Believe me, it feels good. It will feel even better if you've documented your journey up to that point, so that people can see how hard you worked to make it happen. If enough of us start to document, we could completely destroy the myth of the overnight success.

Put your stuff out in public so you have to live up to it. As long as it's valuable and you know it's true, don't judge it. Let the market show you whether you're good or not. There's always something new, and the only way to win is if it's your truth. Just produce. Become that personality, and own it.

Your natural gifts can take you only so far. If you want to be the best, you'll have to work at it, but avoid being a perfectionist. Perfection doesn't exist; it's totally subjective. We earn people's respect and loyalty when we let them see us up close and dirty. Knowing that should ease any misperception that you have to start this process fully formed. Remember, there was a time when Kobe and Beyoncé still had to use their last names.

HOW I'M CRUSHING IT

Rich Roll, Rich Roll Enterprises, LLC

IG: @RICHROLL

It was an ordinary flight of stairs that set Rich Roll on the path to crushing it. The year was 2006, and the thirty-nine-year-old had it all: a lucrative career as an entertainment lawyer, a loving wife who had enjoyed her own success as a fashion and interior designer, four healthy children, and a fabulous home nestled on three acres in Malibu Canyon.

He was miserable.

For years he had blindly chased the promise of the American Dream. He had everything going for him and played the game perfectly. "I got into every college I applied to. Harvard, Princeton . . . I went to Stanford. I was a world-ranked competitive swimmer in college. I graduated from Cornell Law School in 1994. Everything was about, get into the best school, study hard, get into the best law school, get the best law firm job, work hard, show up early, stay late, impress your bosses, get on the partnership track, buy the nice car."

He accomplished all this even while secretly struggling with a debilitating drug-and-alcohol addiction that eventually came close to ruining his life. Yet despite achieving sobriety and all the material trappings of success, the happiness that he had expected remained elusive, landing him in the midst of an existential crisis.

> I'd looked around the law firm, and I didn't aspire to be any of the partners that I saw. I didn't want their lives. It's not that I disrespected them, it's just they didn't have anything that I wanted for myself. And this created a huge problem for me because I had invested so much time and money and energy, years and years of my life, to get to this place, and I felt I was stuck. I didn't know how to get out of it. I'd never stopped to think, *What would make me happy?* Or, *What is it that I'm passionate about?* Because that was just never part of the conversation.

Then, the night before his fortieth birthday, while climbing the stairs of his home, Rich started sweating and had to stop to catch his breath. He realized that the years of junk food and workaholism that had packed fifty extra pounds onto his frame were taking their toll, hurtling him into middle age on course to the same heart disease that had killed his grandfather at a young age. In that moment, his combined health and existential crises propelled him to make a massive lifestyle change.

Literally overnight, he adopted a vegetarian diet and started running. Within two years, with the help of his wife, who was already a healthy-living practitioner with an interest in Eastern healing and spirituality, he had embraced veganism and transformed himself from an overweight couch potato into a world-class ultra-endurance athlete. He had also left the corporate law firm and started his own boutique practice.

> It basically revolutionized every facet of my life physically, mentally, and emotionally. I lost all this weight. My skin cleared up. I felt amazing. I had better mental acuity. I slept better. The sheer fact that I had changed so dramatically in a pretty compressed time period made me realize just how resilient the body is. And I got interested in trying to test the outer boundaries of that for myself. I started to think, *If I could change so dramatically in such a short period of time, what other leaf could I turn over?*

While he felt great about how far he had moved away from the lifestyle choices that had sapped his sense of possibility, he still wasn't sure what it was he was moving toward. If he could have made a living as an endurance athlete, he would have, but he had a family to support and a mortgage to pay, and there was zero money in endurance events.

Or so he thought. After placing high in the 2008 Ultraman World Championship, a double-Ironman, three-day, 320-mile, ultra-endurance event in Hawaii—and becoming the first vegan to finish the race—the media started reaching out for interviews. Everyone wanted to know: how was a forty-two-year-old performing at such incredibly high levels on a completely plant-based diet? It was unheard of. Suddenly Rich became aware that what he was doing might actually be of interest to someone outside his nuclear family.

Rich had a MySpace and a Facebook account and had started using Twitter relatively early, but he was using these "like the average human being." Now aware that people were interested in knowing more about his diet and training regimen, he suggested to a friend that they film themselves as they trained at a camp in Hawaii for the 2009 Ultraman World Championships. "We bought one of those little flip cameras, and we started making daily videos about our training for this crazy race. We were like, 'Let me show you behind the scenes. Here's what I'm eating. Here's how I'm training.' And we would upload these to YouTube, just short little five- or ten-minute super-hacky amateur videos, but they were getting a couple thousand views! I couldn't believe it."

It was while training for this race that Rich read *Crush It!*

I was already starting to see the results of what these social-media tools could do for me, and although I didn't know how they would translate into some kind of tangible career, I believed in their power. And I had faith that by continuing to double down on my devotion to them, at some point it would somehow pay a dividend. [The book] validated everything that was percolating in my mind and gave me a very practical and ultimately very doable road map to move forward. Perhaps even more important, I really took to heart something that Gary made very clear in that book and continues to make clear to this day, which is that you have to have the long view.

I wasn't trying to cash in on a Twitter following to do a brand deal or anything like that. I didn't care about making money on social media. All I wanted to do was deliver valuable content—entertainment, information—that would be helpful to them, without ever looking for anything in return. Because I knew at some point—and that might be years down the line—I would be able to call upon them to come back around for me. In the meantime, all I cared about was trying to cultivate and tend to this flock.

[I wasn't] trying to grow it as big as possible but to make sure that the people who were paying attention to me and had taken the time to follow what I was doing received something of value that would be beneficial in their lives. Approaching it from a professional point of view and shifting my mind-set to that of a practitioner was very powerful and empowering at the same time.

He became more purposeful.

Instead of just being lighthearted and fun about it, I really did think, "OK, what is the purpose of this tweet or this video or this Facebook post? What am I delivering that's gonna be of value?—whether it's a smoothie recipe, a certain sort of strategy about training, . . . [or advice on] how to be a parent and train for a crazy race like this and not get divorced."

The following year, in 2010, Rich completed the EPIC5 Challenge, five Ironman-distance triathlons on five Hawaiian islands in seven days.

He doubled down on blogging and engaging with followers, earning plenty of rebukes from those close to him for being "distracted" and "not present."

Rich's first chance to monetize came about in a way that 100 percent supports my theory that the number of our social-media followers is secondary to the quality of those followers. Rich had been blogging for about four years when he got a call from Sanjay Gupta, chief medical correspondent of CNN. Turns out Gupta had been reading the blog, and he wanted to come to the house for an interview. Rich suddenly realized that his days of anonymity might be over. "I thought, *Oh my God! Millions of people are going see me on CNN. I should have something available on my website for people to buy if they're interested in learning more about how I've done what I've done.* So I literally pulled an all-nighter and created an online cookbook with my wife's amazing vegan recipes." In eighteen hours, he had used his rudimentary Photoshop skills to pull together some photographs and recipes and created an e-book, listing it on his website for nine dollars.

The interview went viral, and the blog post he wrote for CNN was number one on the network's home page for three days straight. That little nine-dollar e-cookbook that Rich edited overnight paid the family mortgage for about two years.

Shortly afterward, Rich was offered a $150,000 contract for his first book, *Finding Ultra.*

I realized that that book was going to be the fulcrum that could leverage my new life completely. So not only did I work incredibly hard to make that the best book possible, but also I worked doubly hard on marketing it once it was done, because I realized, if I didn't put everything that I had into getting that book out there, it would just come and go like so many books. And then I would have to go back to being a lawyer, which was the last thing I wanted to do.

Rich was relentless, writing blog posts for anyone who would let him contribute, appearing on any podcast that would give him a slot, accepting every single interview he could get, and speaking in front of any and every group, even if his audience was only four or five people. He also recruited his social-media community. "I did call upon my audience to say, 'OK, here's this book. Help me get this out. Be my foot soldiers. You guys know how much content I've delivered for you. If you've gotten anything out of anything that I've delivered to you, I'd really appreciate it if you could help me get the word out about this.'"

The day *Finding Ultra* hit the bookstores in 2012 was the day Rich decided he was done practicing law. Sure that he was now positioned to command sizable fees for his appearances, he let his bar membership lapse. Despite his popularity, however, the demand still wasn't there. Without his earnings from the law practice or other consistent revenue streams, even with the money he earned from the book and his speaking engagements, the couple wasn't bringing in enough to support the family long term. The following years were scary and lean.

Because I have a law degree from Cornell and a college degree from Stanford, it'd be very easy for me to backpedal into a cushy, well-paying job. So for me the most difficult part was to say no to that and to stay the course even when we were forty-eight hours away from our home being foreclosed on, even when I couldn't put food on the table, even when my car got repossessed. I made a lot of mistakes, and it could be argued that I was imprudent in some of the decisions that I made; 2013 was a very hard year. There were some dark times when everybody I knew was telling me that I was crazy and that I was being irresponsible.

He managed to secure a short-term job helping a friend launch a media platform for a new eco-business venture in Hawaii and moved the family there. A big podcast fan, Rich launched his own, The Rich Roll Podcast, another platform where he shares his personal insights and gives his audience a chance to hear him discuss issues and ideas with interesting guests. It would become hugely popular and retain a consistent spot in the iTunes podcast Top 10, yet it would be more than two years before it would grow to the point where he could monetize it with ad revenue. All the while, he continued to put out content on his blog and YouTube channel. Rich admits that when he suffered self-doubt and started to question his judgment, it was his wife, Julie, who kept him going. "She kept telling me that I had to do this, urging me not to lose sight of the bigger picture. When I had my dark night of the soul and thought, *This is insane. What am I doing?* she was the one who said, 'You gotta keep going.' We were sleeping in a yurt in Hawaii, and still she'd say, 'We'll work it out.'"

The family moved back to Los Angeles, and things started to turn around. The bank allowed them to renegotiate their mortgage. Rich's audience continued to grow, and he started getting invited to appear on more prominent podcasts. He booked more prestigious speaking engagements for companies like Goldman Sachs. He secured a second book deal, and *The Plantpower Way* was published in the spring of 2015. His reach and popularity has spread so wide, he's now considered "an influencer's influencer."

Rich's story has a fairy-tale happy ending, but he's quick to reiterate that the only reason he is where he is today is because he went all in and had a spouse who was willing to go all in with him. He is deeply aware of the sacrifices and hardship his family endured while they waited for him to find his way.

I had to work my butt off for many years to get to this point. I had to be willing to lose the house to pursue this dream, and reconfigure my relationship to material things. And I could not have done it without Julie; she always held the belief that it was going to work out. We risked everything to be here. Everything. And it was all worth it, but it wasn't easy. To this day, my thirteen-year-old daughter doesn't want to go back to Hawaii because she associates it with trauma. I have two boys, now twenty-one and twenty-two. It was rough, but they were also able to see their parents pursuing what they loved, navigating hardship together. I think something like this could break up marriages and families. In our case, it brought us closer together, and it actually taught the boys an important lesson. Like, look, life is difficult. You just don't get what you want when you want it. The fact that we were able to get through it, and get through it together, was an invaluable lesson to them. And I think that has allowed them to value what we have a little bit more in the longer view. They've said as much to us. I'm wracked with guilt that my daughter associates Hawaii with trauma, but I'm a better parent now than I would be if I had had to go back to being a lawyer just so that I could hold on to a house, so that my daughter won't be upset. What kind of example is that?

I did this because I loved it. I was desperate to find a new way to live. I love doing the podcast. I love writing these books. And now every single day, I get e-mails saying, "You changed my life. You have no idea how much you've influenced me." And I'm sure Gary gets e-mails like that up the wazoo, but to me, the idea that that's where I am now from where I was not that long ago is absolutely shocking and stunning. And it's really entirely attributable to really trying to understand how to become the best practitioner of these incredibly powerful social-media tools that have given me this life that I never thought that I could have.

My advocacy and my message are about the power of transformation. It's about owning your story. It's about the courage to be vulnerable. It's about the innate capacity that we all have to not only change but to tap into reservoirs of potential that are lying dormant. And it's about performance. The fact that I was able to do five Ironmans on five Hawaiian islands in under a week at age forty-four on a plant-based diet speaks to this sort of untapped reservoir of potential that I think we're all sitting on top of, because I don't consider myself to be anything special. And that feat is really just a metaphor for the sorts of things that we all overlook in our own lives that perhaps we should pay more attention to.

In September 2017, Rich completed the ÖTILLÖ Swimrun World Championship, considered one of the most difficult endurance events in the world. During the ÖTILLÖ, which means "island to island" in Swedish, competitors swim and run forty-six miles across twenty-six islands in the Stockholm Archipelago. It took Rich and his teammate almost eleven hours to finish, three hours behind the winning team. In an interview with the *New York Times,* he confessed the race was the hardest thing he had ever done. But he also added that the experience validated one of the important messages he frequently shares with his followers: "The main thing is realizing that even if you feel terrible for a while, that's not how you're going to feel the whole time. . . . Things change if you just keep moving."

4

WHAT'S STOPPING YOU?

Align all eight of the essentials—intent, authenticity, passion, patience, speed, work ethic, ability to track consumer attention and master social platforms, and content—and you have the closest thing to a formula for crushing it that I can offer. Yet I know that even a so-called formula won't be enough to get some of you into do mode. Every day I meet people who swear they are going to start their own "thing." Most won't. I asked my team to give me a list of the most common reasons they've heard, whether in the comments sections of our content or in their interactions with other aspiring entrepreneurs, for failing to crush it. Here's what they came up with:

I have a full-time job.
I don't have any money.
I have kids.
I don't have time.
My industry has too many strict rules.
I have an idea for an app, but I don't know how to code.
My parents don't get it.
My family is holding me back.

I'm afraid my friends will get ahead of me.

I still haven't finished the books assigned by my life coach.

No one was watching.

Only a few people were reading.

I don't know which idea to pursue.

I don't have the right equipment.

I don't know where to start.

I'm too old.

I'm an artist, not a businessperson.

I'm not into anything monetizable.

I'm afraid I'll get hate comments.

Every one of these is bullshit, and some belong in the category of "Are you fucking kidding me?" Of the hundred or so finalists we considered before winnowing the list of *Crushing It!* contributors down to the ones we included in this book, only a handful were bringing in more than a moderate income at the time they decided to go all in and crush it. Many were flat broke or barely making ends meet. Several had young children, and others were old enough to be grandparents. A number had already failed at previous attempts to build businesses. At least three had served jail time. You can write these examples off as anecdotal, but remember, we received so many responses that we couldn't possibly include them all. If hundreds of thousands of people can figure out a way to crush it, isn't it possible that you could, too? Isn't it at least worth a try?

About the hate mail. Yes, there are hateful people out there who are pissed off because they're not doing shit, and you will likely hear from them, especially, as photographer Jared Polin points out, if you succeed. Don't let them keep you quiet, or as Polin also says, "Fuck the naysayers." Sometimes it can be hard, and some people will get more hurtful or inappropriate feedback than others. Women will have a different experience on social media than most men will. Surely you already know that many, many dudes are scum buckets. Then there are the run-of-the-mill insults that can come from anyone: You're ugly. You're stupid. You're not all that. Want to know how the best influencers handle that crap? They ignore it or they confront it. In fact, you probably haven't made it big until you've read aloud your hate mail in a post. Hell, Taylor Swift wrote a number-one song about it. Misogyny, racism, and bigotry are very real problems, but they are not the reason why you're not crushing it yet. *You are the reason why you're not crushing it yet.* For real, when the haters come at you, just shake it the fuck off. You know they're not crushing it because they've got time to waste spewing poison at you. You should pity them. If you really want to show what you're made of, transform their ignorance into phenomenal content for your fans.

Social media and technology haven't made the world any worse than it was before. They don't change us; they expose us. And that's not a bad thing. We're always more effective against the demons we know and can identify than the ones hiding in the dark. **All the reasons people throw out to justify why they're not doing what they say they want to do boil down to one of three kinds of fear**, each of which requires a different response.

Fear of Failure

Well, that's what people say they're afraid of, anyway. I think what they're really afraid of is being judged by people whose opinions mean something to them.

I'm not going to minimize this. I know it well. I don't give a crap what people think, and yet there are days when I will go to ridiculous lengths to turn around someone's negative opinion of me because I care equally what everybody thinks about me. Believe me, I get it, especially if you're worried about justifying yourself to your family. I have the most supportive family in the world, and even I occasionally get razzed when one of my investments fails or something doesn't go the way I predict it will. So I can totally understand how devastating it would be to learn that you've disappointed your mom, earned the scorn of your siblings, or been dismissed by your closest friends. But you are just going to have to find a way to get over it. Get a shrink, start practicing yoga, find a hypnotist, do whatever it takes to settle your nerves, embrace the moment, and stop caring what other people think. Commit to ignoring every single voice that threatens to undermine you. If it's your mom, find a respectful way to tell her you want her love but not her opinion. If it's your friends, tell them you are grateful for their concern but they have to choose to support you or fuck off. The only person you can't ignore is your spouse if you have one. The way around that is to work with your husband or wife to come up with a plan that you can both live with. There will always be people around you to tell you not to do things. **You have to let yourself be your sole judge and jury.**

In my experience, good communication solves all things. I advise everyone in this predicament to confront the problem head-on. Sit down with the people you care most about and say, "I am going to do something I should have done ages ago. The only thing that stopped me was my fear of what you'd say, but you need to know that I'm over that now. I don't need your blessing, but I do need to know that I will have your support when I fail. Because I will. Not spectacularly, I hope, but definitely in the short term. In the long term, though, I'm going to win, and it would mean the world to me to know you've got my back and are hoping for my success, not waiting for my failure."

Then, no matter how they respond, start. Just like that. You'll be amazed how quickly you can work when you're no longer tethered by the tyranny of other people's opinions. People who are afraid to fail will always set their goals far lower than they need to, much to the delight of their competitors.

No one who played it safe ever made it big. This is *your* life, and I promise you the chances of truly ruining it are slim. Short of self-destructive behavior or a complete lack of self-awareness, there is very,

very little you can do that you cannot recover from. Be clear-eyed and strategic, be willing to work harder and longer than you ever have in your life, and you won't disappoint anyone. In fact, I predict you'll surprise everyone.

HOW I'M CRUSHING IT

Rodrigo Tasca, Tasca Studios

IG: DRIGO_WHO

Rodrigo Tasca is not leading the glamorous life. The thirty-one-year-old moved back into his parents' house in Florida to save on rent. He hired his sister to help with his videography business, and his studio was his bedroom. It's a far cry from when he used to live in New York, where he was photographing models and shooting behind-the-scenes videos for magazines. Yet, he still thinks he's got it better than some of his friends. In fact, he feels sorry for them.

"Moving back to Florida was a risk, but I knew that I had to get out of my comfort zone. . . . I wasn't getting any younger. But I was willing to start back at zero and put in the work. I wake up every day and I'm happy with what I'm doing. But then I'm hanging out with some friends and they're just like, 'God, I hate what I'm doing.' Dude, there's no reason why [you should be] doing something that you hate nowadays. But they're afraid to fail, or they're afraid about what their image will look like."

He gets it. It's hard to impress women when you tell them that you're living with your parents. "I'm thirty-one years old, definitely feel like I want to settle down more. But if I meet a girl nowadays, there has to be an understanding. I'm trying to create something bigger here, and I need to make this sacrifice for the next year-and-a-half of my life so I can have a better life, and a potentially better life for us within the next five years. If you're not cool with that, you're not the girl I'm looking for."

Rodrigo started out in the restaurant business, first with his family, later working for a large corporation. About seven years ago, he won a GoPro at a company holiday party raffle. He loved playing around with it and making videos but had no intention of doing anything else with it until he visited a friend of his living in Peru. The friend was a real estate agent, and one day, when his photographer didn't show up, he asked if Rodrigo could take the pictures instead. He agreed but then offered to take some videos of the property, too. He spent the next seven months filming and renting real estate properties in Peru.

Upon his return to the United States, he moved to New York for a short-lived position at one of his previous employer's new restaurants, then paid the bills by working at a tennis club, where he landed his next job as a personal chef for a family in the Hamptons, while also freelancing with a catering company. He discovered *Crush It!* when his company cooked for Techweek 2015 and he heard this Belarusian immigrant tell the story of how he made money as a New Jersey teenager buying Shaq dolls at the dollar store and returning them to Kmart across the street for a full refund. This kind of hustle was familiar to Rodrigo, whose family had moved to the States from Brazil when he was a small child. Money was tight, so when his parents would go to Costco to buy supplies for the restaurant, he'd buy a box of candy bars for six or seven bucks and sell them to his classmates at school for a dollar each.

He'd listen to *Crush It!* during his hour-long subway commute from his apartment in Crown Heights to cook for his clients' family on the Upper East Side, and it convinced him to follow his passion and start filming. Film school was financially out of the question; he was going to have to learn on the job. He started with his roommates, who were models, and then offered to do a shoot for a clothing company where one of his friends worked. They put the shoot up on their Instagram, and it got so much attention that they invited him to shoot another event. He earned a little money for that gig, but it would be the only one that paid out of the next ten or so videos he'd create. And that was by design. While taking so many online Udemy classes that the company contacted him to find out why he was consuming so much content so fast, he was offering his services for free to anyone he could find. "I'd find someone who was having an event, and say, 'Hey, is somebody shooting for you?' And if they said no, I'd offer myself up. It was pretty much, what can I do to get my foot in the door? I didn't have the technical skills, but I figured going out and learning and getting the field experience and the opportunity to work with clients was going to benefit me in the long run, so when I was ready to charge somebody, all those skills from the free stuff I was doing would come into play."

He had the perfect day job to accommodate his training. The family he worked for in the Hamptons and the Upper East Side would have him work about forty hours over two or three days, which left the rest of the week open for him to work on his craft. "You have to start building those connections. That's what drove me. At first it could be discouraging, but Rome wasn't built in a day."

After about three months, he finally got paid $200 to film a behind-the-scenes video for a large publication. Eager to get away from the New York winters, he started researching the Florida market for those types of videos and discovered that there was a void. No one was doing that kind of work down there. He decided he would be the one to create a market for it.

So Rodrigo moved back to Florida in March 2016. Things did not go well.

> In New York, I would find a client and then do the whole project for them, the whole process, shooting a video, editing, and producing. I thought I was going to come back to Florida and be this hotshot from New York, and then I realized that no one cares that I was in New York. It's one of those things; I needed to wake up and realize that the other thing I learned about from *Crush It!* is growing a personal brand. At first, I was like, "Hey, I'm Rodrigo Tasca from Rodrigo Tasca Productions." And everyone is like, "Who?" And pretty much I got a lot of doors shut on me. But then I changed my brand to Tasca Studios, and then people were willing to set up an appointment to meet with me and hear what I had to say, and learn that there was a market for small-business videos versus behind-the-scenes for magazines. So changing that brand was like adjusting to the market, realizing that people didn't want to hire just one guy who does it all, unlike New York, where if you're not the one guy who does it all, they're going to find someone else. There are still clients here who have only recently started a Facebook page.

Rodrigo is committed to helping his clients learn how to market online, teaching them the basics of Facebook, Instagram, and YouTube marketing, even when they resist at first. His persistence and commitment have paid off.

A year ago, when I started, we were calling businesses and offering free videos, and people were like, "No, we're not interested," or "No, we don't need it." Compare that to the fact that I now charge clients twelve hundred dollars for the day to shoot. I'm going to California. I just got back from Tennessee after shooting at a music festival. It's just so crazy that within one year of hard work and hustle—where that has led me.

I could move out, but I'm considering staying at my parents' house for another year and then getting an office space. My family is super supportive about what my sister and I are doing (she left her job and works with me full-time now). They're like, "Whatever we can do to help. We wanna see this work out for you guys." I really wouldn't have made it this far without the support of my friends and family.

Fear of Wasting Time

If you're under the age of thirty-five, this isn't even an issue. You can always go back to the practical world in twenty-four months if you stink or hate what you're doing. School and the nine-to-five grind are not going anywhere.

It bears mentioning that a fear of wasting time has also caused many more-established entrepreneurs to miss important opportunities. There are a lot of people who ceded ground on Instagram because they were putting all their energy into Twitter and Facebook. The people who laughed at Snapchat should feel pretty foolish now. Every platform is worth some investment. Of course not every one will feel like a good fit, and not every platform will pay off, but you can't know until you spend some time there. For every Snapchat and Insta where I won, there was a Socialcam where I lost. I can assure you that whatever I learned on Socialcam made me a hell of a better player everywhere else.

People are so scared they'll be wasting time if they try to build a business, even when their time isn't valuable. If you're sacrificing time you could have spent with loved ones or doing something that brings value to your life—or hell, $50K—then I can see how that might cause you some regrets. But if you're giving up only your downtime— time you would have otherwise spent with *Game of Thrones* or some video games—how can you say it was wasted? You're literally giving up empty hours in favor of doing something that could fill your life with joy, and you're worried about wasting time? That's bullshit. If you're not 100 percent happy with your life today, it is never a waste of time to try something that could get you there.

HOW I'M CRUSHING IT

Sean O'Shea, The Good Dog

IG: @THEGOODDOGTRAINING

When you're young and your biggest dream is to become a professional musician, you accept that you'll be working low-prestige, highly flexible jobs, like bartending and waiting tables, to keep you financially afloat until you make it. It goes with the territory. Everyone's got to pay their dues. At twenty-five, even at thirty, you're cool with it.

At forty, not so much.

For eleven years, Sean O'Shea worked as a valet, parking cars at a restaurant as well as for a company that handled private events for Beverly Hills celebrities. A drummer since the age of three, he'd played on hit records with artists like Alicia Keys, CeeLo Green, Jennifer Hudson, and Ghostface Killah. Despite being a part of some hit tracks, it was the valet work that was paying the bills, not the music. The future was not looking bright, and he was in "a bad space."

His break came in the form of two demented dogs. Both pound puppies, at six months the Chow mix, Junior, and pit-Rhodesian, Oakley, were sweet and cute and everything you want in a puppy. But like a lot of dog owners, Sean didn't really know what he was getting into. Puppies require a lot of consistent training and discipline, and Sean admits he did everything wrong. At first the dogs were just obnoxious and ill-mannered, but by the time they turned two-and-a-half, they were dangerously aggressive and reactive toward other dogs. "We were a menace to the neighborhood. They were huge, and if we were at the park and the grass was wet and they saw another dog, they would literally take off and pull me on my ass, like I was waterskiing, except on my rear across the park. I even ended up on *Judge Judy* because my dog had gone after another person's dog."

He didn't blame the dogs; he knew the failure was his. And he knew that if he was going to keep these animals and protect them, he was going to have to figure out a way to turn things around. He started watching *Dog*

Whisperer with Cesar Millan and studying dog-training techniques. He also started doing some deep personal development work.

"To be honest, I was a pretty good mess. I studied my ass off. Not traditional books, but a lot of personal work to change my belief system, change my values, work on character, work on everything that I had never really received as a kid or as a young adult."

It took a few years, but eventually his methods—known as "balanced training" technique—turned his dogs into models of good behavior, much to the surprise and relief of the neighbors. The transformation was so remarkable that around 2006 he was able to start a neighborhood dog-walking business, supplementing his income as a valet and part-time musician. He became the guy who could take a giant pack of fourteen dogs out at one time and make it look easy. Naturally, people started asking him if he could train their dogs, too. As a valet and musician, he'd brought in about $20K. In his first year of training and walking, he brought in $65K. That figure doubled the second year.

Sean started to feel a new dream coalesce, one that didn't include going on tour with a band. Yet while he had discovered a natural ability to communicate with dogs, he was not a natural businessperson. "I didn't know anything about business. Zero. Like the word *brand*, the word *marketing*—I didn't know anything about any of that stuff." He read obsessively to educate himself, however, which is how he came upon *Crush It!* He followed every word.

"I dove in pretty naïvely, started creating a ton of videos, starting doing a ton of Facebook. I remember simple conversations with myself: *If I was the consumer out there, what would cause me to come back to a Facebook page or a YouTube channel over and over again?* And the only answer I could come up with was if it helped improve my life, if it had value in that sense. And that was my guiding light."

Even though he wasn't comfortable on camera, he started filming videos with a cheap flip cam. "Do-it-yourself videos, a ton of teaching videos, a ton of before-and-after videos, a ton of showing what we could do, but also teaching people how they could do their own thing." Other trainers were doing the same, but his intense efforts and the fact that he was early to the platforms, served to differentiate him and elevate his profile.

A lot of trainers at the time, whether in social media or otherwise, were in a kind of chest-beating space, like, "I've come out of the womb and I instantly was gifted with this thing." My journey was more like, "I fucked everything up, and I was a wreck, and my dogs were a wreck. Here's my journey of how I got out of there. Let me share that with you guys." I was really transparent and doing my very best to try to share the information, the tools, the approach, the techniques, and my own blueprint for how I got out, including personal-development stuff and recommended books.

I worked obsessively. I studied, studied, studied, studied, trying to understand how to do this right and how to build this, because I was so obsessed with doing something special. I finally felt like I found my break. My biggest goal was to do something that had an impact. It sounds cheesy, but that was really where I was at. I think I struggled for so long not feeling that way that when I found the opportunity, I just went kit and caboodle all the way in. I was determined to find my answer, determined to develop, cultivate the skills so I could move forward. And I knew I had a shit ton of catching up to do. I was so far behind.

His following grew quickly. He waited until he was "overflowing" with clients before quitting the valet gig. "I'd been there eleven years, and everyone was like, 'Where do you think you're going?' And I was like, 'We got plans.'"

Within a few years, he had built an international profile (he called in from Scotland for an interview for this book, after speaking in front of the Scottish Parliament about balanced training and his ideas for regulating the industry). In 2012, he opened a second location in New Orleans. He hired a partner, Laura, who had worked with some big names in Hollywood and could provide the administrative and organizational support he needed, and more trainers to handle the increased demand for his services.

Now forty-nine, Sean does very little training himself, except when especially dangerous animals come in, which he takes on until they're safe for his team to work with. People fly their dogs in from all over the country. And trainers travel from all over the world to study with Sean and his team, learning not just training techniques but how to leverage social media for their businesses. He spends about six hours a day creating content and responding to his community. He's also written a book and created DVDs, and he runs a Q&A podcast. "There are so many people around the world who can't get to us and can't get to other trainers for help with serious stuff. We're trying to empower people. We get feedback from people in different countries, and they're sending pictures of their dogs off leash, fully trained, just by using our free videos. It's really awesome."

One thing he hasn't done is product placements. "I

don't want to cheapen the blog. Not that [I wouldn't do it] if something amazing came along. And I don't mean monetarily, necessarily. Money would be great, but there are so many cheesy products from people who don't even build relationships. They just send you an e-mail and they're like, 'Hey, would you put this in your blog?' No!" He has built the entire business through social media and his personal brand. In 2016, he grossed more than $600k.

Not a moment goes by when he's not thinking about the business.

> I have a little bit of downtime, but with Instagram Stories and Instagram and Facebook and YouTube and responding and training and running the business, there's not a whole lot of extra time, but that's cool for right now. It's what's needed in order to get things to the right space. I'm totally down for it. To be honest, being forty years old [when I started], I don't feel I have time to waste. It's not a desperate thing. It's not a freaked-out or panicky thing. It's just, "You don't have time, buddy. You wasted a lot of time doing a lot of stuff that didn't serve you. Let's go hard and see what you can make happen in the time you've got."

Fear of Seeming Vain

When I wrote *Crush It!* in 2009, I got a good amount of grief from critics who accused me of glorifying narcissism. I don't hear much from them anymore, because I've been proven right by the consumer, aka the market: developing a strong personal brand leads to business success. Don't worry about seeming vain. Embrace it. Everybody else who is crushing it did. Remember, smart entrepreneurs don't care what other people think. You'll look like an ass for a while if you walk around with a camera constantly pointed at your face, **but everyone looks like an ass when trying something new.** Reality TV was once a joke, remember? Now you can't turn around without seeing a reality star on a magazine cover, a makeup counter, some exercise equipment, or a frozen-food package. **Everyone's an ass until they're a pioneer.**

Set Your Mind to Success

The most exciting part about being an entrepreneur today is that we're still living in the early years. The pool is crowded, but there is still plenty of room for you. Get in while you can! Look, I'm sympathetic. I didn't learn how to swim until I was nine years old because I was too scared to put my face in the water. The only reason I finally learned was that one day I was playing air hockey at the community pool when I heard my mom clapping and cheering. My younger sister had just figured out how to do the crawl stroke and was making her way across the pool. I ripped off my shirt, threw myself into the pool, and started swimming before my mom's applause stopped echoing. There was no way my sister was going to learn to swim before me.

Sometimes you just have to jump into the pool, even when you're scared.

As you gather your ideas and put your strategies in motion, set yourself up emotionally to succeed. Find your courage and strengthen your self-esteem until you feel brave enough to make some noise and invite people's attention. Then show them that you care deeply about keeping it.

Several of the people interviewed for this book said that, while hugely inspiring, *Crush It!* didn't actually compel them to change anything about how they were growing their personal brand or running their business, because they couldn't imagine operating any other way. Caring about quality, value, and the customer experience above and beyond anything else was already working for them. We live in such a fast, casual, cynical world that it can be almost disorienting to customers when they come into contact with someone whose eagerness to help or please bowls them over like an enthusiastic Saint Bernard. Disorienting but also delightful. And addictive. *Crush It!* merely confirmed what these stellar entrepreneurs already felt deep in their hearts, and it gave them the satisfaction of knowing they were right to follow their instincts.

It's very *Wizard of Oz*, actually. Let me get a little Glinda the Good Witch on you: You've always had the power to achieve your wildest ambitions. There is literally—*literally*—no reason why you can't become an entrepreneur and influencer in 2018. It's my greatest hope that by the end of this book, you'll feel a lot like nine-year-old me as I hurled myself into the deep end of the pool and realized, "Oh, I *can* fucking swim!"

HOW I'M CRUSHING IT

Mimi Goodwin, Mimi G Style

IG: @MIMIGSTYLE

The school of hard knocks is a brutal place to get your formative education. Mimi Goodwin should know. Raised in Chicago by a single mother who worked two full-time jobs to make ends meet, she often spent time at her grandparents' house, where she was molested at a young age by two male family members. When her mother remarried, Mimi was abused by her stepfather. She would find respite every summer in Puerto Rico, where she went to spend time with her father. Her aunt was a seamstress, and Mimi loved to make clothes for her Barbies while sitting next to her as she sewed ball gowns and wedding dresses. Mimi's father bought her a sewing machine, and she took it back with her to Chicago, where her mother would buy her fabric. When she was thirteen, Mimi offered to make a dress for her mother to wear to a wedding. The end result was horrible—the dress's hemline was off and it didn't fit properly. Mimi's mother wore it proudly anyway. Mimi was thrilled, and a seed was planted.

Unfortunately, Mimi's home life became intolerable and she ran away, leaving the sewing machine behind. Seeking year-round warmth, she used money she'd stolen from her mother to buy a train ticket to California, where a friend of hers had moved with his family a month before. "I thought that all of California was Hollywood." She couldn't understand the conductor over the loudspeaker. "I remember the conductor saying 'something, something, California,' so I got off the train. And it ended up leaving me in Pomona. And I was like, 'This doesn't look anything like the movies.'"

For eight or nine months, she lived in a city park, sleeping on a bench or with random people in exchange for money or food. She eventually made her way to her friend's house and moved in. The friend became a boyfriend. She experienced domestic violence there, too, and right before her sixteenth birthday, she found out she was pregnant. Upon hearing she was going to be a grandmother, Mimi's mother came to visit and try to mend the rift between them. "She apologized, and I apologized. I think I had a greater understanding for my mom after I became a parent; I found myself in very similar predicaments."

Eager to give her daughter, Chastidy, a safer living

situation, Mimi moved out of the boyfriend's house but wound up squatting in an abandoned apartment building with no running water. Her mother begged Mimi to let her take the baby until Mimi could get her life together. Reluctantly, she agreed.

Mimi married the first person she could, so she could get a house and bring her daughter home. Again she found herself in an abusive relationship. A second daughter, Lexi, followed in 1998, and Mimi tried to stick it out with her husband, but when Lexi was a few months old, Mimi asked some married friends if she could move in with them. She had a job as a receptionist and soon moved into her own one-bedroom apartment. She was making ends meet, but barely.

> There were weeks where we would have a lot of potatoes or a lot of Top Ramen or whatever we could manage at that time. I would come home from work, go right into the bedroom, close the door, and cry. I felt I was drowning in whatever this life was. And the kids would cry, "Mom! Mom! Mom!" and I'd collect myself and go back into the kitchen and make dinner and move on, because that's just what you do when you're a mom.

Things started looking up. She found a job working as a receptionist at a 3-D digital media company for a man named Steve, who mentored her and educated her about his business. She got married again ("my healthiest relationship"), had two more children, and took up her old hobby, sewing. Her husband turned the garage into a little sewing room for her.

She'd wear some of her handmade clothes to the

office and always get compliments. Her boss, Steve, who was always the first one to scream across the room, "She made that!" would often sit her down to talk about her ambitions and goals. One day, when they were having this conversation and he was asking yet again what she'd like to do besides be a receptionist, she replied, "I think I'd like to be a fashion designer."

"How much would you need?" he asked. They talked further about what steps she would have to take to make her dream come true, and she went home.

The next day, she found a $30,000 check on her desk.

She started working on a collection and even had a runway show at the Fashion Business Institute in Los Angeles, but she realized soon enough that while she loved designing, she hated the other aspects of the job. Steve didn't get upset. "You'll figure it out," he assured her.

In 2012, she noticed that a lot of people were starting sewing blogs and making commercial patterns and crafts at home. She thought, *I can do that*, so in March she started her fashion sewing blog, Mimi G Style. At the time, you could find online instructions to make a quilt or an apron, but there was nowhere to go where you could find out how to make the clothes you saw in magazines. "I would take something I had seen on the runway that of course I could not afford, modify it, and create something new."

One day she made a skirt inspired by a piece she had seen from Oscar de la Renta. She posted it on the blog, and people went nuts, begging her to make one for them. Mimi wasn't interested in sewing for hire, so she posted instructions on the blog. The requests persisted, however. Finally, around Christmastime, when she was thinking about gifts for her daughters, she thought, *What if I just take a couple of orders?* So she posted that she would take orders for twenty-four hours. She priced the skirt high, at $198, to keep the number of orders low. And she warned people not to expect to get their skirt for four weeks. Then she went to bed.

When she woke up the next day, she had thousands of dollars' worth of orders.

She freaked out, sewed nonstop with her daughters cutting and her husband folding next to her, delivered the skirts, and swore, "Never again." Then she thought, *What if I could just teach them to make it themselves?*

She filmed a series of video lessons, showing people step-by-step how to create a garment from scratch based on their body measurements. She created one new video per month, and earnings rose so fast that in two years she was able to quit her job and focus on growing her business. Meanwhile, "I was getting all these e-mails from everywhere in the world, from all these women saying, 'I came across your blog and you inspired me to start a new hobby,' or 'You're inspiring me to dress better,' or 'I just lost my job,' 'I'm going through a divorce,' 'I was thinking of committing suicide,' or 'I'm in rehab,' and then saying things like, 'Somehow your blog has helped me get through.' At that moment, I realized that the blog was less about fashion and sewing and really was a vehicle of motivation."

A friend who loved business books introduced Mimi to *Crush It!* in 2015. By then, her blog was trucking along, she was developing her own products, and she had started her own line of commercial patterns. She was already using and loving social media, but reading the book showed her that there was still more she could do. "OK, you turned your hobby into your career, it's your passion, you're working hard, but now you need to do more. Now you need to engage more. Now you need to crank up your customer service. Now you need to spend time asking all these questions and making sure that those followers and those fans really engage and become loyal to you. You need to keep building that community."

For example, one day Mimi posted that she was going fabric shopping, and someone wrote that she would be willing to fly all the way from Tampa to go fabric shopping with her. "I thought that was insane, but I moved the date by thirty days, and people came! And at the end of the day, they asked, 'What are we doing next year?' Next year?"

The next year, she booked a hotel, set up some classes, and about eighty people showed up. In 2017, the Mimi G Style Fashion Sewing & Style Conference celebrated its sixth anniversary. It's followed by thousands of people on Facebook, Instagram, and Mimi's blog.

Mimi has worked with about three hundred different brands by now, but she says the day she got a call from *Project Runway* was her greatest moment.

They were working on *Project Runway Junior*, and the kids were going to be using vintage patterns and turning them into a more modern look. They contacted Simplicity [Pattern] because they knew that's what I used, and asked if I could come on the show and be a mentor to the kids and introduce the challenge with Tim Gunn. And so the folks at Simplicity called me and said, "Hey, *Project Runway* called. They want you to come do the show," and I was like, "*What?* Yeah, let's do it!

When Mimi read *Crush It!*, she was excited to learn that there was a term for the type of business she was running—*a reactionary business*. She's still at it, looking ahead to see where she should go next. She spotted a big hole and is now in the process of filling it.

In the sewing community, I've been able to cross all boundaries. I've been in every sewing magazine that there is. I've been very fortunate. But I'm Latina, and a lot of my community is African American or Latino, and when I looked in those sewing magazines, there's nobody that represents us. I got to a point where I really wanted to see more of myself in these magazines, and I thought, *Well, I'll just do it myself.* We launched *Sew Sew Def*, a digital multicultural sewing magazine that focuses on both men and women and will feature a lot of makers from all walks of life.

As soon as we launched it, it got a lot of amazing reviews. People were posting and sharing it because there wasn't anything like that. And for me, I think that the more people I help, the more I get back. I've been very fortunate that I get to work with all of these brands, but not a lot of makers do, especially those who look like me. I know that there are so many, because they follow me, and I follow them and see their work. If I can bring awareness to them and get more of the brands that I work with to have a better representation of the entire sewing community, not just a part of the community, then I've done my job.

5

THE ONLY THING YOU NEED TO GIVE YOURSELF TO CRUSH IT

PERMISSION

www.garyvaynerchuk.com/permission

HOW I'M CRUSHING IT

Pat Flynn, Smart Passive Income

IG: @PATFLYNN

Pat Flynn had planned to be an architect since the days when he was a straight-A high school student. After graduating magna cum laude from UC-Berkeley, he quickly landed a job with a renowned architectural firm in the Bay Area, where he became one of the youngest people ever to become job captain. His future bright, his 401k growing, he proposed to his girlfriend, who said yes. It was March 2008.

You know what happened next.

Three months later, Pat lost his job, along with 2.5 million other people in the country that year. It was a huge blow. Pat had even gone the extra mile to become accredited in Leadership in Energy and Environmental Design (LEED), a professional credential that proves mastery in the highly specialized area of green building. The LEED AP exam is so rigorous, it has only about a 30 percent pass rate. His bosses had assured him that the certification would look good on his résumé and factor favorably into his annual reviews. Eager to impress people and differentiate himself from the competition, Pat studied during much of 2007 and the early months of 2008 to prepare for the test. Overwhelmed by the mountain of material—the reference guide alone was more than four hundred pages—he created a website to keep himself organized and make it easy for him to cross-link and access his resources and notes from wherever he happened to be, because he traveled so much for work. He took the exam in March 2008 and passed with high marks. That's when he got promoted to job captain.

Because he was in that role, he was given a few months to wrap up his projects before his job ended. That bought him a little time to shrink his expenses and get ready to live extra lean. He and his fiancée moved back in with their respective parents, and Pat started calling everyone he knew in the industry, and every contractor or mechanical firm he'd ever worked with through his employer, to beg for a job. No one was hiring. A fat lot of good all that studying had done him. A vague sense of depression started to settle in.

In the meantime, he still had to show up for work. Normally he listened to his music playlist during his morning commute—he was taking the train, which was cheaper than driving—but one day he got bored with it and started poking around the podcast selections. He stumbled on the Internet Business Mastery show, hosted by Jeremy Frandsen and Jason Van Orden. That day they were interviewing someone who was making six figures a year helping people pass something called a project management exam. Pat thought about his website. Aside from sharing it with a few coworkers, once he passed the exam in early 2008, he'd mostly forgotten about it. He thought, *I've passed the LEED exam. Maybe I could create something people could use.* So he went to his site. Still not sure how he was going to monetize it, he installed some traffic analytics to prepare for whatever marketing he figured he'd eventually come up with. It didn't take him long to see that thousands of people were visiting to help themselves to the information already there.

He activated the comments section, and sure enough, people started asking questions. He knew the answers.

While interacting with his visitors, he started spending hours engaging with people in other architecture, LEED, and sustainable-building forums, leaving trails to bring them back to his website. At the end of July, he added Google AdSense to his website. By the end of the first day that the site was Google Ad enabled, he had earned $1.18. "It was the most incredible feeling ever. This could actually work! Obviously, you could find that amount of money in the couch cushions, and I couldn't live off $1.18 per day, but it was a sign to me to keep trying. *Who else out there is doing this thing, and where can I get some advice?*"

The hosts of the podcast that had inspired Pat to monetize his website had launched a formal "mastermind" program, as outlined in Napoleon Hill's 1937 self-help classic, *Think and Grow Rich*, to help walk people through the steps of building an online business. One of the founders moved to San Diego, where Pat was living with his parents, and agreed to host an in-person group meeting where people could talk about their process. Pat decided to join them, meeting at a Panera Bread not far from his parents' house. "I felt I had nothing to add, nothing to contribute. I just wanted to be a fly on the wall and listen. And then everybody was introducing themselves and talking about what they had going on. And I was so impressed. It was really inspiring."

It was also really intimidating, and as it came close to being his turn to talk, he got so nervous that he started sweating and having trouble breathing. They asked him to explain what he was up to, and he told them that he'd just gotten laid off but he had a website that helped people pass the LEED exam. They had no idea what that was.

And I'm like, "Yeah, see, nobody knows about this. This isn't going to work out very well."

And they said, "Well, that sounds interesting and very niche. What's your traffic like?"

I said, "Oh, you know, a couple thousand people."

"That's pretty good, you know. Two thousand people a month? You could work with that."

And I was like, "No, two thousand a day."

Whaaaat?

They were stunned. "You're not monetizing this? You don't have an e-book?"

And I said, "I don't know what that means."

The group spent the next thirty minutes explaining to Pat what he could and should do.

It took about a month-and-a-half of working day and night for Pat to write his e-book, which was a compilation of much of the same information that was on the website, but better organized and easier to read, complete with charts. His mentor explained what tools he could use to turn it into a PDF and sell it online (he used one called e-Junkie). He put a graphic on the sidebar of the site, a PayPal button, and a little description of the book, which he priced at $19.99. At this point, he was a week-and-a-half away from joblessness. His sole comfort was knowing that if this didn't work—and he was pretty sure it wouldn't—his parents had promised they wouldn't kick him out.

It was two a.m. when he went live. Pat went to bed, and when he woke up four hours later to get ready to work, he checked to see if he had gotten any sales. Nothing.

"I thought, *God, this is worthless. I wasted all that time.* And then I gave myself an out. It was still early. Nobody was buying study guides at three a.m." So he took the train to work, arriving around eight-thirty a.m. He checked his e-mails. Nothing.

> I was starting to despair, and then fifteen minutes later, I got a notification of payment received for $19.99 minus the fee to PayPal. It was the coolest e-mail I ever received. Then immediately after the rush, I started thinking, *Crap, what if he returns it? What if he doesn't like it? What if he sues me because the information is wrong?*—all this negative stuff that most people feel when they do something outside their comfort zone. So, I go outside for a walk, because I'm hyperventilating, and I come back fifteen minutes later, and there's another e-mail from PayPal saying that I had made a sale.
>
> So even when I was out on a walk, I was making another sale, and that just blew my mind. Like, holy crap, this thing is now available to people 24/7/365, and I don't have to be there in order to actually make the transaction happen. Between the book and the ads on my site, I ended up generating $7,908.55 that month, which was two-and-a-half times more than my architecture income.

There were a few ups and downs, but from that day on for the most part, Pat's income grew month after month. He became known as a LEED expert because no one else was providing the help people were seeking. All that work he had put into the website was paying off. By March 2009, he was bringing in $25,000 to $35,000 per month.

Along with questions about the LEED exam, Pat started

getting requests for information about how he had built his site and business. He remembered all the business gurus he'd looked up, the sites he'd explored, and the newsletters he'd subscribed to when he was trying to figure out how to get started himself. He recalled how he'd felt that they were doing a bait and switch, luring him in with big promises but ultimately delivering very little useful information. "I wanted somebody to be up front and honest with me, but I felt that they just wanted my money."

So he launched SmartPassiveIncome.com, a site where he could document everything he had learned about starting an online business.

Two things happened that made him realize that these websites were not destined to be temporary income generators to keep him afloat until he could get his architecture career back on track.

The first thing was a phone call. About two months after Pat launched SmartPassiveIncome.com, his old boss got in touch. He had been let go from the prominent architecture firm as well and had started his own company. He'd invited a number of Pat's old colleagues to join him, and he wanted Pat to come work for him, too. He offered a higher salary than Pat had been earning at the old firm, a private office, and a year's rent. All Pat had to do was move back to Irvine and pick up where he left off. "It didn't take me more than two or three seconds to say, 'No, thank you.' And when I hung up, I thought about his offer and was very surprised that I had answered so quickly. Why? It was a sign that this was the direction I wanted to go, and I needed to really own it. I wanted to become an entrepreneur."

The second thing was that he discovered *Crush It!*, which helped him come to terms with what had to happen next. "The book says, 'If you want to make money selling worms, do it, and own it, and be that guy.' The LEED exam stuff? Those were my worms. I was that guy."

It wasn't just reading the text of *Crush It!* that influenced how Pat ran his business. Visiting the book's Amazon page, Pat noticed something else.

Gary was actually replying to the occasional negative reviewer and saying, "Hey, I'm sorry this book didn't speak to you. Let's get on the phone and chat." I couldn't believe that an author was paying attention, responding to comments, and offering a phone or Skype number. Many of the one- or two-star reviewers came back with a follow-up comment. They might not have changed their opinion, but they'd say, "Gary, I still don't agree with you, but I so appreciate the time you took to reach out to me and understand where I was coming from." That impressed me more than even the content of the book itself. Where is the ROI in responding to a one-star comment? I saw that (a) he took the time, (b) he cared enough to reach out, and (c) he cared to see what he could do to improve.

After that, Pat adopted the same response strategy to any negative comments he received, and the ROI has been clear. "Sometimes those people with whom I've talked on calls just misunderstood something I said and have gone on to become some of my biggest fans."

Right around this time, Pat's earnings show a striking upward inflection point. "I'm not saying that *Crush It!* was the sole reason why I was able to grow my income to what it is now, but I went bigger, that's for sure. I started to produce more things instead of being just a blogger.

I started to look for other ways to expand beyond my realm of comfort."

And expand he did. He started a YouTube channel in 2009. In 2010, he launched the Smart Passive Income podcast, which has seen more than forty million downloads. In 2011, he started accepting offers to speak. To provide a space to answer the deluge of questions he gets from his followers, he then created a daily Ask Pat podcast, as well as a few others to address niche subjects. His self-published book was a *Wall Street Journal* best seller.

All along, he followed through on his commitment of being a "crash test dummy" for online business development. He started creating new businesses live in front of people—like a site for people interested in starting food trucks and one for people interested in becoming security guards—and posting his revenue for those, too. If he made a mistake, he made it in public. He detailed every step of the process along the way. In the end, Pat's passion for architecture and design was surpassed by his passion for helping others.

I'm getting e-mails from people, paragraphs long, thanking me for helping them save time and effort or for helping them get a promotion. I've gotten handwritten letters from people I've helped pass the exam. The interesting thing is that in October 2009, I asked people why they had bought the e-book from me. I thought the information would be useful so I could continue to do whatever it was they were going to tell me was working. About a quarter of those who responded said things like, "Pat"—that was another cool thing; they were calling me by name, as if they knew me—"Pat, I bought from you because you finally gave me an opportunity to pay you back. I didn't even need the book; I've already passed the exam. But you provided me so much information, I felt I needed a way to give back to you." I eventually learned that this reciprocity is human nature, and I was setting up systems for that kind of interaction and transaction.

The great thing about Pat's success is how many options it affords him. He has been expanding his philanthropic reach, and he serves on the board of an educational nonprofit. He's interested in getting involved in shaping education policy. Despite his belief in *Crush It!*, he isn't trying to be another GaryVee. "I am who I am and he is who he is. That's what *Crush It!* is also about, you know: being confident in who you are, not trying to be like somebody else. When you really own it, and you put yourself out there and be you, your vibe is going to attract your tribe, and you're going to be able to make change in this world."

Pat's story is waiting to be told a thousand more times. I know many of you have niche expertise, yet you don't think it could possibly be a real business. But come on! I mean, the LEED exam? Are you kidding me? If Pat Flynn can make a stellar income off a website dedicated to helping people pass an exam only a few people in the country have ever heard of, you can do it with soccer trivia or smoothies. Please dig deep into what you know best or what you love most, or better yet, what you know best *and* love most, and start creating content. Follow the blueprint Pat's story provides; go deep, go niche, and provide real value in the form of entertainment or information.

Though it may seem that, over the years, influencers

have had their pick of thousands of platforms they could use to establish their brands, you need only both hands and a few toes to count the number that actually had the ability to grow big enough to scale. It's really, really hard for a platform to earn a spot in this book. If I've included it, it's because it's grown into such a beast, it cannot be ignored, or because I see the potential for it to become that kind of beast. When considering where to build your personal brand, you want to use nothing less than platforms upon which you can actually build your life. Every platform we discuss in the following pages fits that description.

II

CREATE YOUR PILLAR

6

FIRST, DO THIS

No matter what kind of influencer you want to become, everyone must start with this step: create a Facebook business page.

Facebook is the cost of entry to building a personal brand. Do not try to tell me that you don't have to do it because you're targeting the twenty-two-and-unders, who are not on Facebook in the same numbers as older groups. As you'll see, the strides Facebook is making in video make it likely that it's about to become more appealing to those young viewers. You want to be waiting for them when they start opening Facebook accounts. Facebook will get to the young demo; you can count on it. Don't ever underestimate Mark Zuckerberg, and don't ever bet against Facebook.

HOW I'M CRUSHING IT

Costa Kapothanasis, Costa Oil—10 Minute Oil Change

IG: @COSTAKAPO

Constantine "Costa" Kapothanasis sounds like a practical man. The first-generation Greek American from

Portland, Maine, won a Division 1 baseball scholarship to a college in Maryland. Forced to give up the sport professionally after a shoulder injury, he moved on to earn a master of science in finance. After graduation, he worked for several large financial companies, but nothing stuck. "I either got fired or was almost fired from every job." He chafed against bureaucracy. Not only did these large firms force him to follow strict, cumbersome protocols that to him seemed inefficient and counterproductive, but also their restrictive social-media policies hampered his side business of making custom, hand-carved baseball bats. Bank trading hours were 9:30 a.m. to 4:00 p.m., and Costa found himself missing opportunities because he couldn't respond right away to potential customers on Twitter, which was enjoying its heyday. It didn't help that, as the years went on, friends from his baseball days made it to the majors and were making millions playing the game they loved, while he was sitting in a cubicle. Many years went by in which he avoided watching baseball on television.

He needed to plan an escape, so while still working for the financial firm, he sold the assets to the baseball bat business and bought a quick-lube, a place where you take your car for a fast oil change. It wasn't the most glamorous or exciting business, but he saw it as an investment in a "quasi-utility," almost like electricity or water: in a car-dependent country with few mass transit options, most Americans will eventually need an oil change. Then, as was almost inevitable, he got fired. It was fantastic! "Getting fired was this amazing thing for me. My quality of life went through the roof. I never realized how much of a weight was on me, and now it was gone, and it put me into high gear to do something with the business."

Costa went all in on his quick-lube company, which he named Quick Change Oil, but his strategies weren't all that effective. Direct mail. Search-engine optimization. An iHeartRadio commercial that was before its time. He wasted a lot of money. He found himself about eight months later alone in the store on New Year's Day, 2016, because he had given his employees the day off. Sales were not great, and he was in a tough spot. Nothing was going on, so he was reading a book called *Crush It!* The more he read, the more he thought, *Man, I need to do this*.

No more direct mail, no more SEO, no more commercials. Instead, he took to YouTube, and in between cars and after work until two a.m., he taught himself about Facebook ads. "I didn't want to storytell incorrectly. I didn't want to miss an opportunity."

By February, 100 percent of his marketing budget was devoted to Facebook ads, and he was immersed in social engagement and creating content. He used Twitter searches to find any vehicle-related conversations that would give him a chance to talk to people. From Chevy Cobalts to Porsches, he photographed his customers' cars for Instagram, tricking the images out with photo filters to make them look snazzy and sharp (customers like seeing their cars online so much, he doesn't have to ask them for permission anymore—they ask him to do it first). He started putting out educational videos to help inform potential customers about the ins and outs of their cars. "We have put out videos on the different types of oils, the difference between a full-synthetic and a conventional, on when you should do an engine flush. And we've gotten lots of feedback. People will type messages like, 'This is the first time anyone has actually explained to me what the purpose of my air filter is.' I truly believe that the most educated customer will always pick us."

Less than a year after that New Year's Day when he sat in his empty shop wondering how he was going to jump-start his business, he had six store locations and was under contract for two more, spread out over several states. Today he's busy running the business, keeping his social-media engagement up and staying genuine, creating content, and appearing on various financial TV and radio shows to talk about his journey. He was even invited to speak at a university entrepreneurship program. He and his wife are talking about starting a family. He's been working on building his personal brand, too—in 2017, all the businesses were renamed Costa Oil—10 Minute Oil Change.

7

GET DISCOVERED

You need to understand something: when you're starting with nothing, you will find that your absolute breakthrough opportunities will be developed in two ways:

1. By the smart use of hashtags, a strategy that requires an unbelievably long grind.
2. By direct-messaging, i.e., reaching out directly to people and offering something of value in return for their attention, a strategy that requires an unbelievably long grind.

It's the second one that I believe holds the most promise, which is why, whenever possible, I've included instructions on how to collaborate and business-develop within each platform we discuss in this book. Collaborations are the absolutely most tried-and-true way to grow a fan base quickly—*quickly* being a relative term. **In most cases, you should count on this process taking years, not months. If that bothers you, close the book.**

Many are uncomfortable with the idea of direct-messaging total strangers, but let me help you think about these total strangers another way. Let's say a friend invites you to join a group for dinner at a restaurant, and she also brings a couple you don't know. You wind up sitting next to each other and have a great time. You're an interior designer, and you find out that this couple is in the beginning stages of deciding to redo their home. Do you hide the fact that you're an interior designer? Of course not. It's natural to tell them what you do for a living, and that's going to become part of your conversation because you just discovered a mutual interest. Now, at the end of the evening, would it be weird to hand them your card and say, "Check out my website, maybe we can work together. Or let me know if you need other recommendations." Of course not. You have a mutual interest, they need a service, you can provide that service. It follows that you should give them the opportunity to decide if you would be a good fit.

Online, social-media platforms are the mutual friends connecting you to millions of people that share your interest in interior design. Your job is to do the research and find out which would find the most value in your offer and then make your case. I'll share with you the specific details on how to do this in upcoming chapters, but the general process is essentially the same on each platform: reach out, make an offer they can't refuse, and get to work producing something that doesn't make them regret giving you a chance.

Now, there's something you should know: right this minute I have around five hundred DMs from people who want something from me. You know what I have to say to them? Mazel tov, and go away. And that's if I'm in the mood to be nice.

Why would I encourage you to try to get other influencers' attention when I ignore or reject the majority of people who try this tactic with me? Because if they were doing it right, I wouldn't reject them. If I felt they weren't just trying to use me, if I thought they were genuinely trying to be helpful, if they could recognize a hole in my business and had the knowledge and skills to fill it, I might consider talking to them.

When you can't offer exposure or money, what do you have? Knowledge and skill. Do you own a pizza shop? You could offer free pizza from your shop for six months. Are you a graphic designer? You could offer to make six hundred custom filters. Do you own a liquor store? As soon as your targets post shots of themselves enjoying wine, you could direct-message them with an offer for a case a month for the rest of the year (if your state laws allow that—New Jersey doesn't ☹). People will tell you not to sell yourself cheap, but you can stand on that principle only when people are willing to buy what you're selling. (For a perfect example of how to do this right, read DRock's story in chapter 3 of my book *#AskGaryVee*, or you can hear his version of the story in his *Medium* piece, "How I Got My Job for Gary Vaynerchuk.")*

If established influencers see an upside to collaborating with you—allowing you to post content on their pages, working together to create content—they'll get back in touch. If not, they'll say no thanks, usually by not answering. But if you reach out for six or seven hours a day, you will eventually find someone willing to try something new with you. Once you do, you'll have raised awareness with thousands of people who previously didn't know you were alive. Provide something valuable to your collab partner, and you'll quickly raise your profile as an influencer and in all likelihood make a new friend.

I won't lie. Biz-deving this way is hard, tedious, and time-consuming. I like tedious. It means most people won't do it. If you do, you will win. If you've got the money to run ads on all these platforms or pay influencers to feature your product, more power to you. But if you're just starting out and have no money, this is the number-one thing you can do to build your brand.

---

* You can read his version: DRock, "How I Got My Job for Gary Vaynerchuk," *Medium*, June 1, 2017, https://medium.com/@DavidRockNyc/let-me-preface-this -story-with-something-ive-been-thinking-about-lately-2242480640f2.

MUSICAL.LY

I'm going to start with Musical.ly because I'm betting that unless you're the parent of a seven-to-eleven-year-old, you've never heard of it. If you have, I'm betting most of you never once thought it might be worth investigating for any other reason than checking on your kid's online activities. Musical.ly, like a lot of its users, is young and creative and eager to grow up. It's a fun platform to consider, because I think it's the one most likely to be underestimated. It's also the one most likely to no longer exist once you read this book, because as of this writing, its popularity has been in decline for about six months. But you need to learn about it anyway, for reasons that should become clear in the next few paragraphs.

Despite the evidence that platforms that start out hot with young people can and do successfully cross over to an older audience, the majority of entrepreneurs will still dismiss Musical.ly, which is great, because it leaves the platform wide open for you to take it over. You'll have fun doing it, too. Musers, as the users of Musical.ly are called, have turned this app into a creative phenomenon. Originally, it allowed people to make fifteen-second lip-sync videos, making public the rock-star impersonations and glamming that previous generations used to do in front of their full-length closet mirrors. Today the form has evolved to include original music, comedy skits, and even mini–educational videos. Ballerinas, makeup artists, gymnasts, jugglers, athletes, rappers, vloggers, and hams of all stripes—including Jiff the Pomeranian—are using the medium to show off their skills and style. You can create content as long as five minutes, compile video clips into stories, and collaborate on duets with other musers.

The company saw immediate favor among the tween and teen crowd as soon as it launched in August 2014, with people not only downloading it, but returning to it and engaging in high numbers. For the first months of its existence, it grew, but at a slow, steady pace. Then the designers decided to make a few minor changes to the app design, one of which included relocating the Musical.ly logo so that it wasn't cropped out every time a video was shared on Instagram or Twitter. As soon as that happened, new users flooded the app. Learning from the mistakes of its predecessors, which too often tried to contain users to their platforms, it helps musers build their fan base by allowing them to share its content on Instagram, Twitter, Facebook, and WhatsApp. It now has 200 million users, 30 percent of whom spend thirty minutes or more there per day.

No doubt a small percentage of musers are refugees from Vine, the defunct Twitter-owned six-second-video platform that was quickly overshadowed by Instagram video and Snapchat, thanks to their slightly longer formats and fun editing tools. The natural question is, of course, how will Musical.ly avoid Vine's fate? One way is by aging up, creating features that appeal to their audience once those kids become teens, so they don't graduate to Snapchat or Insta. And it will have to evolve to compete for the younger audience, too, as Snapchat and Insta start trending younger and younger. The way I see it, for Musical.ly to break away from its competition and gain momentum within the twelve-to-seventeen-year-old crowd, it will have to pivot the way Facebook did a few years ago, when it successfully transitioned into a mobile-first platform even though it was originally designed for desktop. Musical.ly is so young, it should be limber and flexible enough to be able to adapt itself to whatever is the next big thing that changes the platform paradigm. Maybe it'll be voice. Maybe it'll be something that we can't even envision yet.

Clearly, emerging musicians have a natural opportunity here, but of course one of the best ways to become a big fish is to swim in a small pool, creatively adapting a platform to your needs. That's the tactic I used to build brand awareness on Musical.ly. You might wonder why I, a forty-two-year-old businessman with few ties to the music industry, have any interest in garnering attention on a platform geared toward thirteen-year-olds. Simple: those thirteen-year-olds grow up to become eighteen-year-old entrepreneurs and twenty-five-year-old marketers. When I was twelve and dreaming of building businesses, no one knew what to call me. *Entrepreneur* wasn't part of our lexicon. Today, entrepreneurs are pop-culture icons, and the kids are growing up watching *Shark Tank*. Maybe I can help inspire them to get where they want to go faster. Maybe one day we'll do business together.

One of my earliest forays into the platform came about because I thought kids could get some value from hearing sage words from hip-hop artist Fat Joe on #AskGaryVee. To help the demographic find the show, I posted a clip of me jumping through the ceiling, set to Fat Joe's "All the Way Up," with the hope that if they liked what they saw, they'd keep watching and listening. If they did, they'd catch the meme I created from a clip of me pushing hard work, set to Rihanna's song "Work," or an inspirational video reminding people to always look up to the stars, set to Coldplay's "A Sky Full of Stars." I made another one of me remembering how much I hated school, how I'd sit in the classroom thinking that one day I would prove all my teachers and classmates who thought I was a loser wrong. Imagine how much that message might mean to a kid who's getting the same shit today? What if just a few of those kids see it and realize there's someone out there who gets them, and they find out what I've accomplished and think, *Yeah. Me too.* This is how someone like me, who's not in the music industry and can't sing, managed to tie business and entrepreneurship into a so called lip-syncing platform, not only to make a difference but to make fans for life.

Even before I deployed these content strategies, however, when I was just gathering information so I could figure out how to build out my profile, I asked two of Musical.ly's top users to make guest appearances on #AskGaryVee. On episode 198, I'm flanked by two fifteen-year-olds, Ariel Martin and Ariana Trejos. Definitely not my typical guests, but we had a blast. My audience and I got access to their insights, and they got the chance to show their skills on a big YouTube show. The thing is, my show is peanuts compared to the big venues where they've appeared, like the red carpet at the People's Choice Awards. The real value to me is that when their fans Google them and find the Musical.ly memes they made while on my show, it will raise their awareness of my brand. When Baby Ariel is a humongous star (in 2017 she was listed in *Time* magazine's third annual list of most influential people on the Internet), I'll have the content that the world is hunting for in a few years when they want to see who she was in her early days.*

Even if Musical.ly turns out to be a fad, let us remember that every season, brands pay millions of dollars to run ads against pilots for new series, most of which statistically will not exist after nine months. As of 2012, 65 percent of new shows are canceled after one season. It literally does not matter how long a platform lasts. What matters is that it exists. If you're seeking to build your audience, go where the audience goes, wherever that may lead. Consume the platform's content for a couple of weeks to get a feel for what's appealing to users, then

---

* I hesitate to offer parenting advice, but if you're a parent with a talented child, this might not be a bad place to let him or her showcase their talents. You're never too young to start building a personal brand. Can you imagine if Justin Bieber's mom had banned him from YouTube? Maybe manager Scooter Braun or some other talent scout would have discovered him anyway. But maybe they wouldn't have, and now Bieber could be just another physical therapist with a beautiful voice who'd always have to wonder, "What if?"

strategize how you can create content that will successfully penetrate that market. Get to know it and put your resources into it. Not all, mind you. Just some. More if you're comfortable with the platform, less if you decide it's not for you. But to label any platform as irrelevant shows a lack of imagination and vision. Don't ever doubt that the designers of the platform have a greater vision for it than whatever it is you see now. Platforms evolve, either by design or by accident, when the market takes them in a whole other direction. If you get in early, you can evolve with a platform. Become a real presence on it, and its designers may even come to you and ask for your help. For example, they may give you early beta program access, letting you play around with new features they're hoping to launch. Or you could get first dibs on creating fresh new content in a format or style no one has ever seen before, essentially creating a symbiotic relationship between your brand and the platform.

No one can finish a marathon without proper training. Whether you do it on the treadmill or the running path, you have to get to know your body, build your endurance, and figure out what physical, nutritional, and psychological practices extract your best performance. The same goes for social-media platforms. In 2012, I was bullish about an app called Socialcam that was successful for maybe nine months before it flopped. In those nine months, however, I learned strategies that served me well when Vine and Instagram came along.

The only thing you risk by taking leaps into the social-media unknown is time. You want to break out and live the life? You say you're going to die if you have to spend one more day in your accounting job, but you're not willing to risk your time in case a platform turns out to be a MySpace or a Vine instead of a Facebook or an Instagram? Who are you to be so fancy? When you're nothing but a beggar, you don't get to be choosy. Download every new social platform, taste it, and understand it. Drop it if it doesn't work for you or you can't get comfortable, but never reject anything without educating yourself about it first (which is good advice for like, life).

Musical.ly 101

Work those hashtags. I can't believe we didn't talk about hashtags in *Crush It!* In fact, I didn't mention them in print until my third book! Riding hashtags is one of the bedrocks of social media and a key to discoverability. One of the quickest ways to build traction on Musical.ly, for example, would be to open the app, examine the trending tags on the Discover page, and work on producing great content around those trending tags so that you can be spotted by kids who would otherwise have no way to know you're worth checking out. That includes the curators at Musical.ly itself, who are apt to reward good content by selecting it to be automatically featured when people open the app. That hand curation creates more random opportunities for you to be seen than you might find on other platforms. Don't count on winning this virtual lottery ticket as your shortcut to stardom, though. The amount of hard work and creativity you apply to your content will be a much better predictor of your success. You can also create amazing content coupled with your own clever, original hashtags. Knowing your way around hashtag culture is an excellent way to give your quality content longevity and legs.

Collaborate. There was a time when the whole appeal of stars was their untouchable quality. It gave them mystery and cachet, and if we did actually get access to them, in the form of, say, an autographed photo, that meant a lot. But today's stars are measured by their approachability, and they can pay a serious price if they get too Hollywood. Take advantage of this. There is nothing stopping lyricists or songwriters from uploading their creations, direct-messaging top musers, and giving them a chance to lip-sync or even perform their material. You could do the same thing with a funny skit, or a poem, or some other work. I've said it ad nauseam: the best way to reach out to a community is to become part of a community. Engage, comment, share, and create without asking anyone for anything. Become part of the community, and you'll have a much better chance of getting someone to create a meme using your material, or better yet, create your own meme that other people fall in love with and share.

That doesn't mean that if your brand would be appealing to twelve-to-seventeen-year-old girls, you shouldn't spend any money on Musical.ly. It's just that in this one man's point of view, the top 1 to 2 percent of influencers on any platform are often overpriced. Not always; you might get lucky and find some who are great deals because, despite having the most reach, they've underpriced themselves. But eventually people get wise, so don't count on it. Regardless, the enormous opportunity for marketers can be found in the middle and long tail of influencers. So if my brand were really attractive to tweens and young teens, I would spend 40 percent of my overall marketing budget on Musical.ly, and 40–70 percent of that amount directly on arranging deals with Musical.ly celebrities. The rest I would use to experiment with programmatic auction ads. Then I'd watch closely to see which performed better, adjusting as I go.

Musical.ly is the perfect place for a performance-oriented person to sell a performance, but it's also a place where a performance-oriented person can sell pencils, or açaí juice, or fidget spinners. An artist could make a video of himself painting or drawing, set to music. A writer can make a video that evokes her mood for the day. I make inspirational and motivational memes out of larger pieces of pillar content; my best hits have been made by clipping a word or phrase from one of my rants and setting it to music. Wanna hear me speak Russian? Check out my "Hustle" Musical.ly video. Also, see how I managed to link my ALS ice-bucket challenge to Gwen Stefani's "The Sweet Escape." That's probably the best singing I ever did in my life.

Creative people can be creative anywhere, and the most creative people do it where no one else has tried before. More often than not, people who produce content for people like themselves often hit their mark better than people who are one step away from their audience. I do well with alpha guys because I have alpha male DNA. I'm also hugely empathetic, so I can also deeply connect with emotionally intelligent people who are patient enough to get past the alpha DNA. A dancer intuitively knows how to produce content for other dancers; someone who has transformed his life through self-development knows how to reach others seeking a similar epiphany. Your creativity will be the variable to your success on this platform—and any other.

Imagine This

Let's say that after working for years as a professional singer and actor, you decided that you were done pursuing stardom and made the choice instead to take over your family's summer camp, located in the woods just outside the limits of your hometown. This is an exciting move. Imagine, you are finally going to stay in a home long enough to invest in some real furniture and get a dog. And you aren't leaving the industry entirely; you plan to add more acting and musical theater classes to the camp so you can continue to share your passion and expertise. You smile as you imagine the all-camp variety show at the end of each summer session.

Unfortunately, you didn't take over a thriving business. While once yours was one of the only camps of this kind in town, over the last decade or so, several more have been established here and in surrounding areas, and business has gone down. In particular, summer camp registrations are nowhere near where you think they should be. Once you had to drop a session because too few children enrolled. You've tried everything you can think of to grow the business, but compared to the newer, fancier options to choose from, your camp seems a little nerdy and old-fashioned.

While you're hanging out with your eleven-year-old niece one day, she shows you a video of herself lip-syncing. It's the weirdest thing you've ever seen—a fifteen-second closeup clip in which your niece bops around, sometimes backward, making duck faces and shooting hand signals to Kesha's "Praying." It's like an excerpt from a music video. You ask if her mom knows she's playing around on a site where anyone can see her. "Sure," your niece replies. "All of my friends are on it. It's just a place to sing and dance."

A social-media platform embraced by eleven-year-olds who love to sing and dance. What's this thing called again?

You set up a Musical.ly account and start filming yourself performing your favorite songs. You ask your campers to help you pick the song, and you let them direct you. They're impressed—for an old person, you don't look or sound half bad when singing their music. (For the record, you're thirty-five.) You're not even lip-syncing, you're the real deal, straight up. You create micro–music videos that not only showcase your talent, but also the camp. You film from a different location every day—the boathouse, the pagoda, the archery field, the arts and crafts pavilion, and of course, the amphitheater.

One of the girls asks if she can film herself with your phone. You send home a permission slip asking parents' consent to let the kids make Musical.ly videos on the camp account. They know their children are already there, and most agree. From then on, every day, a new camper gets to produce four pieces of content for the camp Musical.ly account. Kids are fighting for their chance to be Muser of the Day; it becomes the biggest reward they can get, and all the kids start working extra hard to be helpful to earn their time. There's an added benefit to letting the kids control your platform: it's a great learning strategy. Instead of figuring out for yourself what kids want to see on Musical.ly, you let the nine-to-eleven-year-olds show you. You now get to watch them, take note of their behaviors, and get a sense of how they think about hashtags and trending topics. Again with the parents' permission, you let the kids document their camp Olympics, scavenger hunt, final campfire, and all the camp traditions that have marked the summers for three generations.

Every child who makes a Musical.ly video immediately tags his or her friends so they can see it. The kids also show it to their parents and their parents' friends. They show it off at school when classes start again in the fall. Over the course of the year, awareness of your

Musical.ly page and the camp slowly begins to rise. By spring, when parents start thinking about which camps to register their children for, the name of your camp is fresh in their minds. You seal the deal when the kids inform their parents that they've all decided they want to attend camp together during the same session.

You become the most popular, fun, hip camp director ever, and your popularity soars, along with awareness of the camp you run. Registrations double, and your performing arts classes are so popular you start to offer them during the rest of the year. You initiate a music video class, which includes teaching the kids the steps to famous music video routines. Within five to eight years, the camp is just one of the summer options available through your new city-based school for performing arts. You're a smaller star than you'd once hoped to be, but you've never been happier.

HOW I'M CRUSHING IT

Chithra Durgam, DDS, Aesthetic Dental

IG: DRDURGAM

Dr. Chithra Durgam has accomplished the near impossible—she's made it fun to go to the dentist. How else can you explain the fact that many of her first-time clients call her at the request of their children? Let me explain.

When Chithra started her private practice in 2004, she did what most medical practitioners do to get referrals: she sent out direct-mail pieces to let her northern New Jersey neighbors know she was open for business. Social media, she thought, was for personal use. It wasn't until she started following a social-media expert online, and then read his book *Crush It!*, that her thinking shifted and she understood how building a personal brand on social media could help grow a business. She was intrigued but hesitated to start. Doctors and dentists are constrained by a lot of HIPAA rules, and "we tend to be overly concerned about what each other thinks about the marketing we're doing." But she gave it a lot of thought and decided that "instead of using my free time to go golfing, if I'm using that time to interact with my patients, and educate people in a fun way about dentistry, there can't be anything wrong with that. And so I kind of just took a leap of faith."

For years, she has spent four to five hours every day, her lunch hour and the time she has after her two boys go to bed, on social media, engaging, reacting, and educating. She has a presence on all the usual suspects—Twitter, Facebook, Instagram, and she has written posts for *Medium*—but what sets Chithra apart from almost anyone over the age of twenty-five, and certainly from any medical practitioner, is that she's on Musical.ly, too. And that's why so many kids beg their parents to bring them to see her.

She creates lip-synced music videos about different procedures, like tooth whitening. She does PSA announcements about healthy eating, mouthing the words of a spoof version of Ed Sheeran's "Shape of You." Sometimes she posts an educational clip, like the one pointing out the difference between a porcelain crown and a veneer. She dances. She does comedy, often in a white jacket, sometimes wielding a toothbrush. She's goofy and awkward, and while that might be all she was, were she just another muser, the fact that she's a forty-four-year-old dentist makes the whole deal pretty hilarious. The comments and responses she gets from the young users there are overwhelmingly positive, and two of her clips were featured by the platform. Her young patients, the ones in the Musical.ly age bracket, follow her. They bring their phones to school and show their friends. And their friends say, "Mom, look at this video. I want to go to this dentist."

Chithra gets a similar response from Snapchat, where she creates content tailored for a slightly older crowd. There she has a weekly series called The Office, modeled after the hit television show of the same name. She and members of her staff have also staged scenes from *Charlie's Angels* and created snaps and stories using Bitmojis, music, and props. She used to try to document, but her audience responded so positively to her creative work that now she focuses on that instead.

Many of the people who find her on Musical.ly and Snapchat can't come to her office because they live too far away, but on Instagram, where she can target more locally, she has a higher conversion rate; people DM her for appointments all the time. In the year since she got serious about pumping out consistent, quality content to these three platforms in addition to all the others, not just every so often, she has seen a 30 percent increase in new patients, with three to four inquiries about braces and whitening procedures per day coming in via DM.

Not only that, Lew Leone, vice president and general manager of WNYW-FOX 5, saw her on Snapchat and invited her to come to *Good Day New York* to talk about flossing after an Associated Press report published that it may be unnecessary. For the record, Dr. Durgam is pro-flossing.

Since then she's been invited to speak about personal

branding at meetings and on podcasts. She is currently working with different brands to help them develop ideas to promote their products through social media, and she has received inquiries from other dentists and doctors asking her for social-media consults, too. "I have taken time to learn all aspects of developing a brand before pursuing this work. I understand that I do have something valuable to offer."

Most of her professional colleagues still don't get it.

I've actually gotten a lot of pushback from people and other businesses. They want a return on their efforts right away; they don't understand why I'm investing time. They don't understand that social media is a long game and that it's about developing a brand as much as it is about selling a product. And if nothing else, at least you develop rapport with people who come to your business. But they don't really see that. So it's been a little lonely because I'm doing work that I believe in even though those people around me may not agree with my methods.

Even some of her clients wonder how she has time to put out so many videos. "And then I'll have to say, my staff and I are very serious about our work, but when we're not working, we would rather spend our free time interacting with patients and educating them, as opposed to doing something that's only in our self-interest. Once I've explained our intention, it's been fine. I'm kind of going against everybody else right now, but I think over time people will understand social media is very important to business."

One of the reasons I'm so excited about this book is

because when I wrote *Crush It!*, I didn't have access to a lot of examples of other people using the platforms the way I was. I was just too early. But now, armed with stories like Chithra's, I can suffocate all of your excuses. Until ten minutes ago, you might not have even heard of Musical.ly; now you know that a dentist is out there using it and other platforms to build her business. That's awesome! Education and execution are the keys to this new world.

SNAPCHAT

Despite its 173 million daily active users (DAU), its 10 billion daily video views, its 2.5 billion daily snaps, and the approximately 18 visits it enjoys from its DAU per day, Snapchat remains another massively underestimated platform. Let me clue you in to an important tell: when the "normals," that is, the nontech, nonbusiness crowd, are the first to start spending inordinate amounts of time on a platform, that's the signal to start paying close attention. That's what drew me to Musical.ly early on, and it's why I knew Snapchat had an exciting future when it first came out in 2011. I saw it as the first social network to closely re-create the way we communicate face-to-face.

Its founders, Evan Spiegel and Bobby Murphy, conceived it as the anti-Facebook, a photo-sharing app for spontaneous, imperfect, and impermanent content. When Snapchat first came on the scene in 2011, the messaging app's vertical video and left-right swiping had people totally confused. It took most users, even the young, a few minutes to click around and get used to it. For teens, though, it was worth figuring out, because it addressed two universal adolescent realities: (1) You don't want to hang where you mom hangs out, and (2) You want to lock your room. Because adults didn't get it, because images "self-destructed" one to ten seconds after being opened, and because it gave you the option of drawing and writing text or captions on top of your pictures, the kids were quick to see its potential as texting 2.0—a freer, less curated, and less dangerous place than other platforms to share and creatively express themselves. And share they did; it became widely derided and even feared as the next sexting tool for the high school set (though it never really was a sexting app; that was just the media jumping on a select few cases and running with the attention-grabbing headlines). Today people don't talk about sexting and Snapchat in the same breath anymore, just as people stopped sneering at Twitter for being the place where attention hogs posted what they ate for lunch, and at Facebook for being a place where college students shared their beer-pong pics.

Today the Snapchat app allows you to post video as well as photos and has added all kinds of extras, like filters, Geofilters, lenses, emojis, and video-editing tools like slo-mo. Content is no longer ephemeral. You could always hack by taking screenshots of images to save them, but with the addition of Memories, which stores your content on the app's servers, Snapchat essentially caved in to the human desire to save and revisit the important moments of our lives. The game-changing introduction, however, and the one that would turn out to have the most influence on influencers, was Stories, a function that allows you to link a series of videos and photos to tell a longer narrative, visible to the whole Snapchat community for twenty-four hours. It arrived in 2013, and I very publicly pronounced it a dud.

You can watch me make my blunder emphatically and passionately at the LeWeb'13 conference on YouTube. I loved the platform, but I thought the change introduced too much friction in the UI and betrayed the whole point of the app, which was to create snack-size disappearing content. I was dead wrong. The Story feature became the main place where users could consume content at scale. Less than a year later, 40 percent of American teenagers were using Snapchat daily. I learned an important lesson from that bad call on Snapchat:

a devoted, sticky fan base is willing to be patient as you experiment your way to the next iteration. The next big launch, Discover, saw Snapchat graduate into a bona fide media platform by offering a page where users would find a slew of brands like National Geographic, T-Mobile, and ESPN. Snapchat now had access to advertising revenue, and that meant so did anyone who could crack the Snapchat code.

The man who did that is named DJ Khaled, but before I introduce him, we're going to reminisce about Ashton Kutcher. He wasn't the first star on Twitter—big shout-out to MC Hammer (joined in May 2007) and LeVar Burton (joined in December 2008)—but after joining in January 2009, Kutcher was the first celebrity to truly scale his brand through the platform. Like Hammer and Burton, he'd been building his brand through talent and hustle for decades as a model, a sitcom and film actor, and a producer and director for the reality-TV show *Punk'd*. I often talk about Kutcher when I talk about the history of Twitter, because it was only four months after joining that he became the first Twitter user to boast one million followers, thanks to a brilliant campaign of challenging CNN to a race to hit the milestone. Suddenly Twitter, which had seemed like a joke to most people, was mainstream.

DJ Khaled created the Ashton Kutcher moment for Snapchat. For over two decades, he built a name for himself in the music industry as a Miami-based DJ, producer, and radio host. Khaled joined Snapchat in the fall of 2015, snapping inspirational and motivational "keys" to life and success. His fondness for the platform, he wrote in his memoir, *The Keys*, was that, "It's not about the angle or editing or lighting or how good you look, it's just you for ten seconds being real with your fans." That authenticity had earned him a sizable fan base. By November or December of that year, anyone following social media could see that whatever it was he was doing, it was something special. Thousands of kids were showing up to meet his bus in places like Des Moines, Iowa. You could start to feel that the scale of Snapchat was shifting. Then, in December of that year, Khaled left a friend's house by jet ski, only to get caught off guard by the waning early-winter light. Disoriented in the now pitch-black water, he proceeded to snap his entire ordeal until he finally made it back to shore. By the next day, his popularity—and his personal brand—had exploded. DJ Khaled made it official: Snapchat was now a star-making vehicle.

So how did Khaled do it? How does a grown-up become famous on a platform that serves as a communication tool among tweens and teens? By not overthinking anything. Unpolished content is native to Snapchat, and Khaled just was who he was. Some people might call such banal, spontaneous content dumb and worthless, but that would be like saying that the minutiae of our lives are dumb and worthless. They're not. When combined, those raw, unfiltered moments make up who we are. We don't judge mundane behavior as dumb when we interact with people; we save such judgment for truly dumb behavior. We accept people in their natural habitats, and we understand that every word people utter is not going to be movie script–worthy. Snapchat is simply a channel that captures that unvarnished reality. The only reason some people think what gets shared there is dumb is because it's on a screen, and we've been conditioned to think that anything on a screen has to be perfectly produced and performed. On Twitter we're expected to be clever or politically astute and insightful. Facebook is where we show off our families and vacations. On Instagram we build relationships through images and short videos. Snapchat, though, is where we put our throwaway content. It's a relief to many because it demands little of either its content creators or users. It eliminated the great barrier to many social networks, which is the anxiety of wondering what you're going to post next, whether it will be well received, and whether it could come back to haunt you one day. With the freedom to post anything, people could experiment and get comfortable building their personal brands without fear of repercussions. That opened the floodgates for many to unleash their creativity and discover and develop new skills. More than one person has left a corporate job or fledgling startup because playing around on

Snapchat led them to create a new art medium or become an influencer, which attracted brands eager to pay them tens of thousands of dollars to promote their products in Snapchat Stories.

It is staggering how many families are filming their days and building actual fame. It's especially easy if you're willing to include your children. That's an extremely personal choice, but babies and cute animals always win, hands down. Kerry Robinson learned that when she used Snapchat to film herself engaging in #salontalk with her baby girl, Jayde, while Jayde took to her mom's hair with a brush. Her Stories on Facebook went viral and garnered articles and TV segments in national media, from CBS News to *Essence* magazine. Today Jayde has her own ad-supported YouTube channel with seventy-four thousand subscribers and an Instagram account with more than two hundred thousand followers. You can watch a video of her opening a gift of children's products from a hair care company and see a photo that expresses thanks for a T-shirt sent by a company that celebrates children with naturally curly hair. You couldn't get a purer example of a person who is famous—and, it would seem, earning money—for simply being herself. That's what can come from posting a single piece of excellent content. What will come of Jayde's online celebrity in the long term remains to be seen, of course, but at a time when people are desperate for good news and uplifting, heartwarming content, a glimpse of your ordinary life could be just what they're looking for.

Many people who have already gotten some brand traction and are becoming influencers, including some featured in this book, stopped producing content on Snapchat as soon as Instagram Stories came out in August 2016. The thinking was that Snapchat is toast. Why bother?

You bother because it's a mistake to give up one of the tools in your tool belt for no reason. Hear this: Instagram and Snapchat are not the same. As always, people are looking for different things on each. Why would you deprive them? Sure, it's hard. That's the challenge. But that's also the opportunity. Because it's hard, only one in twenty of you is going to do it well. You should be busting your ass to be that one in twenty. I understand that you want to focus on what is giving you the best returns right now, but what if it doesn't always? And why would you turn your back on a potentially whole new audience?

As I write this book, I'm constantly checking the App Store to see which platforms are ranked highest. Snapchat is often in the top five. That means it's not an irrelevant platform, and no influencer is too good for it.

If anything, this app is one of the most valuable for anyone whose brand is starting to scale. Much of your competition has surely become too reliant and focused on Instagram, which means those potential eyeballs still on Snapchat are looking for more content to feed them. Make sure you're the one to deliver it. It is so easy for influencers to become sucked into the vortex of the media machine they've created. You risk becoming a caricature of yourself, especially on Instagram, where the images are so highly curated. As a feature within your Instagram ecosystem, Instagram Stories are almost required to stay within the lines and support the narrative you've created there. Snapchat, on the other hand, is an entity unto its own. You can use it to break away from the familiar narrative and show sides of yourself that simply don't exist anywhere else. It gives you differentiated content. Whereas all your other channels intertwine with each other to support your pillar content, Snapchat stands alone. That's an excellent reason in and of itself to take it seriously, even when its DNA makes it a natural draw for the mundane and the silly. It gives you a place to be surprising and different, often in the most ordinary, banal ways. (This is advice I should take to heart, too; I could do an even better job there myself!)

Snapchat 101

Back to the original question: how should grown-ups build their brands and dreams on a communication tool for tweens and teens?

Some people, like baby Jayde, have so much charisma that they're going to go viral the minute they present themselves or their work in public. But those individuals are few. For the vast majority, it will take talent plus a combination of tactics and strategy to get noticed. Yet Snapchat limits those tactics. There are no hashtags, for example, so no discoverability. What that means is that building a brand on Snapchat is truly a test of your branding prowess. It's not about running ads and quantifying every click and mathematical variable; it's about hacking culture. Snapchat reveals who's good at it and who's not. This is why you shouldn't wonder whether to bother with Snapchat now that Instagram has its own version of Stories. Whether or not Snapchat can compete over time, it's a terrific training ground to become a superior marketer and branding expert, not just a conversion-based digital salesperson.

Let me say that again another way. The business world is separated into two camps, conversion-based salespeople and branding-and-marketing people. The former are short-term players; the latter, long-term. With no disrespect meant toward sales, I always try to teach you to be branding-and-marketing people, because the great, life-changing upside resides in long-term thinking, not in figuring out how to make a quick buck. For example, Lauryn Evarts, creator of The Skinny Confidential, takes a long-term view of her investment in Snapchat.

> I answer every single snap I get, and sometimes I get two hundred a day. I sit down at night for an hour and in the morning for an hour, and answer every single question. It's almost like text-messaging your readers like they're your friends. I think it allowed people to really come into my life and allowed me to come into theirs. It's just a different way of being social. And it allows me to tell a story, and while I tell that story, I'm 100 percent providing value to the audience.
>
> For instance, if I go to cryotherapy, I take a picture of where

I am, and then I show me in the booth freezing my ass off. And then I can show what I wore, and after that, I Snapchat the little flier with the benefits. So what my followers get out of that is where to go, what the benefits are, what they should wear, and what it looks like when you're in the chamber. With every single thing I do, I try to hit those four points. I'm not just going to post a picture of my coffee cup. I'm going to say, "Today, I'm drinking iced coffee. I'm drinking it with a silicone straw because it's BPA free, and I like cinnamon in it because it helps with your blood sugar." Every single snap needs to leave them with something or else it's narcissistic.

With Instagram Stories, you're competing with a lot of people. Snapchat has white noise, and whenever I see white noise, I'm intrigued, because that's the way to stand out. Some of these influencers have just been taking pictures for the last five years. Snapchat forces you to show your personality. Are you intelligent, are you funny? What are you bringing to the table other than what you're wearing?

The thing to remember is that no one is famous only on Snapchat. Because of the temporary nature of the majority of the content, the only way to allow it to live long enough for people to discover and get to know you is to cross-pollinate with other platforms. For example, if you missed DJ Khaled's jet ski drama, you can still find it on YouTube. Same with Kerry and Jayde Robinson's salon talk. That means that to be a Snapchat influencer, you need to be strong on the other platforms as well. The content you produce for Snapchat has to be powerful enough to draw views on YouTube, Facebook, and Instagram.

The way to get discovered on Snapchat is not much different from the way television stations try to get people to tune in to their programs, which is to market in all the other places where people who might be interested in you are already going. That's what I did. I was never concerned by the lack of discoverability on Snapchat, because

I could see that all I had to do was draw awareness to it through my base on Twitter, YouTube, and my website. I did not use tactics like running Facebook ads to convert people. Instead, I branded and marketed. You'll be in the minority if you're able to figure out a formula that works equally well across platforms—most people lean heavily on the one or two they're most comfortable with—and that rare skill could make you a dominant force here.

All you're doing when testing discovery strategies is figuring out how to siphon people's attention. For example, if you want to bring awareness to your Snapchat profile and you send out lots of e-mails, add your snapcode to the e-mail. Pretty easy, right? You could wear a T-shirt with your snapcode printed on it, or you could create custom Geofilters, which are still underpriced.* Both tactics would allow you to put your brand right in front of people's eyes in a fun, interactive, unobtrusive way.

Snapchat 201

Collaborate. There is no discoverability on Snapchat; people have to know who you are and be motivated to come find you and follow you. That makes organizing collaborations tricky unless you reach out to people on their other platforms—their e-mail, their Instagram, whatever—and either suggest doing something special together on Snapchat or offer something valuable in return for a shout-out or endorsement on their channel. If you need other influencers to help you grow your account, you're probably not big enough to be of much interest to them unless you've got something pretty spectacular up your sleeve. Here are some ideas for growing your followers to build your brand and make yourself more attractive for collabs:

---

* For explicit instructions on how to create and upload your own, read my blog post called "How to Create and Use Snapchat's New Custom Geofilters," https://www .garyvaynerchuk.com/how-to-create-and-use-snapchats-new-custom-geofilters.

▶ Write multiple blog posts about Snapchat, so when the media need a quote about it, they come to you.

▶ Gain visibility by creating Snapchat events, such as the Jurasnap Park project that helped launch the career of Shonduras (see page 167)

▶ Pay for a Google Ad that asks something like "Who Should I Follow on Snapchat?" and offers a list of names, with yours at the top.

One more suggestion: you could visit The11thsecond.com, a website founded by Cyrene Quiamco, also known as CyreneQ, snapchat artist and influencer extraordinaire. She created the website in response to the app's lack of discovery. There you can submit and check out Snapchatter descriptions and user names to make it easier for users to find accounts that match your interests, like Meowchickenfish, who uses Snapchat art to teach sign language, and Snapchatchef, who makes cooking videos. The site is a screenshot repository for cool Snapchat art, as well as a resource where Snapchatters can look for tips, hacks, inspiration, advice, and more. CyreneQ saw a problem—no discovery option on her favorite platform—and solved it. Like all good entrepreneurs, she found a way.

Imagine This

Let's say you're like me, a forty-two-year-old influencer who has become somewhat pigeonholed in terms of the kind of content that's expected of you. You already have a blog, a Q&A show, and a daily vlog. While playing around on Snapchat, you realize that it could provide you with an interesting outlet where you could create a new narrative, a place to microvlog. It's the place where you can talk about your coffee, show a picture of the colorful cereal aisle at your supermarket, and reveal that your favorite color marker is green. It's where Rick the clothing store manager snaps himself playing Wiffle Ball with friends, and where Sally the real estate agent admits that even though she's paleo, she has a weakness for fried pies. Sharing these minor, seemingly unimportant details—often embellished with colorful doodles or fun filters—will do nothing whatsoever to help build any of our brands as influencers in our respective fields, but it does give our followers a chance to see us at our most human.

HOW I'M CRUSHING IT

Shaun McBride, Shonduras

IG:@SHONDURAS

It's no secret that I think spending four years getting a college degree if you have your heart set on becoming a businessperson or entrepreneur is a waste of time and money.

Make that a *fucking* waste of time and money. I feel that strongly about it.

However, I am grateful to Weber State University in Utah, because that's where Shaun McBride received *Crush It!* as a reading assignment from one of his professors in 2010. If he hadn't, it might have been a few more years before we finally heard of him. The timing, however, put Shaun in a position to become a mega-influencer. And he did it on a platform where most people said it couldn't be done.

Shaun embodies the work-hard–work-smart model. At the time that he was getting his degree, Shaun was also running a skate/snowboard shop. It made sense; until then, skateboarding had been his main joy in life. His other love was motivating people and sharing positivity.

He'd spent two years on a service mission in Honduras—that's how he got his nickname, Shonduras—where he had been moved by his experience serving others and helping make a difference in their lives. The skate shop was an ideal place for him to share his love for sport and service. Problem was, while he liked the work, it wasn't always much fun. He knew he wanted to build a business, and he knew his passion was skateboarding, but he had a suspicion that building a business around that passion could be a great way to ensure that he rarely got to indulge in it, like the music teacher and his neglected symphony in *Mr. Holland's Opus*. "You can kill your passions. On a very good snow day, I was in the shop because everyone needed to buy gear to go snowboarding. I think it's often best to chase things that are in line with your passions but aren't exactly your passion."

Upon reading *Crush It!*, he applied some of what he learned to his in-store customer service, but more significant, the book made him realize that if he went about it creatively, he might be able to build an e-commerce business that would allow him to have fun every day doing something he loved. He didn't know anything about e-commerce, but he figured the best way to learn was to just go for it. What could he sell online that would also allow him to interact regularly with people? His first thought, of course, was skateboards and snowboards. But snowboards need a lot of storage and are costly to ship and hard to buy in bulk. They were his passion, but they were not a practical choice. So what was small, lightweight, and easy to buy in bulk?

Jewelry.

Who bought jewelry?

Moms.

And where were moms hanging out?

Facebook.

At the time, Facebook was still in the early stages of its gargantuan growth, adding millions of users every month, women leading the way to make up 57 percent of the site membership and accounting for 62 percent of the shares. And Facebook had all these features that could enhance engagement. For example, if one person commented on a post, all their friends could see it! It's hard to remember, but at the time that was still pretty remarkable.

Facebook became Shaun's storefront and his design studio.

"I would ask my fans to tell me what kind of styles they wanted and help me name the pieces. I'd do giveaways like, 'Whoever picks the best name for this necklace will get ten free necklaces.'" Engagement went through the roof. He gave people every opportunity to interact with the site. "It felt like they were part of the jewelry boutique and that we were creating it together."

No one was more surprised by the venture's success than Shaun.

"I didn't even think it was going to work. I was hoping I could make fifty bucks a week extra by shipping a couple of necklaces out of the back of my skate shop. And within one week, I had more orders than I could handle. Within two weeks, I'd hired all my sisters, and I was paying them with necklaces."

It took only two months to net six figures.

He quickly hired more help, and by the end of the first year, the business had made $1.2 million. But Shaun wasn't there to celebrate. He was having a blast, but after about eight months, he was done. His excitement for the business was rooted in the steep learning curve; now that he'd learned everything he needed to know, he was ready to see if he could apply that knowledge to a new business, one that traded in helping brands tell stories and spread positive messages via social media rather than selling consumer goods. Shaun sold the business to his partner and quit his day job at the retail shop, but instead of immediately starting a new company, he accepted a dream job as a sales rep for some of his favorite skateboard and snowboard brands, a position that gave him plenty of opportunity to "shred" as much as he liked. It also bought him the time he needed to study the market and figure out a scalable, long-term business idea.

The job required that he travel a lot, so Shaun's high-school-age sisters asked him to download a new app popular among teens called Snapchat to make it easier for him to share his adventures with them. There it was: the answer he'd been seeking. At the time, you had to hold your finger on the screen or the image would disappear. That meant 100 percent engagement. You could draw cartoons and doodles on your pictures with your finger, something you couldn't do on any other platform. That meant fun. If there's one thing Shaun had learned from his jewelry-boutique experiment, it's that he was good at creating safe online communities where people could come together to engage and have fun.

"The greatest challenge was trying to grow on a platform that did not cater to growth. Snapchat was a communication platform, like text messaging, so I had to make it into a content-creating platform. Eventually, Snapchat made updates, which helped with that, but I had to get creative at first."

There's a reason Shaun's content got so much attention when so many others on Snapchat did not: he treated

Snapchat like a business. Many people start pumping out cool content onto a platform and just hope they'll get noticed and grow their audience enough that brands will come calling. Usually you have to be more proactive than that. Shaun had a plan. He set himself a series of goals, and everything he did from that moment was in service of meeting them.

Goal number one was to grow an audience through creative engagement and collaborations, so he started doodling. Every day he would post a video of himself doing something goofy or a fun picture he'd doctored to make people laugh, like a unicorn vomiting rainbows over a snowy landscape or his dachshunds in silly costumes and poses. He also invited his fans to participate in his snaps. For example, he drew himself as a triceratops and announced that he wanted help building Jurasnap Park, posting requests for friends to take selfies, draw themselves as dinosaurs, and send the pictures to him. He took screenshots of the images and displayed them. The response was tremendous. "It felt like one-to-one communication. On a lot of social media, you make a beautiful image, and then people comment below. Snapchat felt more collaborative. We built the stories up together."

Most people would naturally assume that it was Shaun's artistic abilities that drew him to the platform, but there's something funny about the way he drew his way to Snapchat stardom.

I literally did not know how to draw. When I decided to make the Snapchat thing work, I thought, "Well, if I want to tell a good story, and I think this is a great platform that's emerging, a lot of it has to do with doodling and creativity, I need to learn." I literally Googled

"How to draw dinosaurs" and then "How do I do angry eyes?" and then I'd put them on my dinosaur. I never copied anything, but I would teach myself how to draw by looking up art on the Internet, and then I slowly learned how to layer things. Give me a Snapchat and I'll make you a funny little doodle, but give me a pen and paper or a paintbrush, and I probably can't do much for you.

He reached out to a talented Snapchat artist, Michael Platco, who was getting a lot of engagement, and with the aim of mutually growing each one's fan base, they created the first Snapchat collaboration: a boxing match. Each invited his fans to send his opponent "punches" in the form of snaps doodled with a colorful *Kapow!* or two, with fists and boxing gloves. The person who received the most punches would be KO'd. Within an hour, thousands of punches were thrown, and Shonduras and MPlatco responded to each round with selfies doodled to make themselves look pummeled to a pulp. They finally declared the fight a draw, but regardless, Shaun had won by multiplying his audience by thousands, making it possible for him to move forward with the next stage of his plan.

Goal number two was to get press. The major hindrance to growing a brand on Snapchat was its impermanence. There was no way to link, no way to share, and the content vaporized after twenty-four hours. The only way Snapchatters could give their content a longer lifespan and establish a permanent online presence was to screen-shoot the images and push them onto Twitter and Instagram. The other way, it occurred to Shaun, was to get someone to write about him. Snapchat didn't even have a website, so the only way someone could learn more about the platform was through Google. Shonduras intended to be the first name to pop up.

Once again, he got creative. His mother, understandably proud of her son, had contacted a media outlet and suggested they feature his work. Concerned that journalists wouldn't pay attention to a self-promoter, he decided to use his mom's e-mail address to pitch stories about Snapchat. Every night, he'd ask his assistant in the Philippines to draft personalized e-mails to contacts at the tech trades—*Mashable*, *BuzzFeed*, and *Business Insider*, for example—with an attachment of his work. The e-mails were written in his mother's voice: "I saw your recent article about YouTube and I thought a story on this new platform called Snapchat might be a good fit for your audience. My son does these really interesting stories there. . . ." In the morning he'd wake up to three or four e-mails from people asking his mom for Shaun's number.

The media attention snowballed until he started getting featured in *Time*, *Forbes*, and *Fast Company*. That kept him relevant and top of mind, so when brands started wondering how they could use the platform, as predicted, his was the first name they thought of.

While all this was happening, Shaun had also been working on goal number three: to tell a story for a brand. "Every brand I've spoken to, they aren't just a product, they have a story, and they want to share it." All along, he'd been hitting up small brands and local businesses to see if they would give him a chance to create some work for them as a case study that he could then use as a marketing tool. No one was interested until he wrote to Disney. Unbelievably, Disney, the biggest brand of all, said yes. Their branding slogan that year was "Show your

Disney side," so Shaun's idea was to go to every part of Disneyland to look for his Disney side, snapping and doodling as he went along. Was he more of a Toon guy, a Tomorrowland guy, or an Adventureland guy? (In the end, he was an Everything guy, snapping a photo of himself sporting doodled Tarzan dreads, a robot arm, Tinker Bell on his shoulder, and a Captain Hook wig.)

From there, the branding work took off. Besides reprising his role as brand ambassador several times for Disney, Shaun has created Snapchat content for Red Bull, Xfinity Mobile, Taco Bell, and many other companies. He even got to help promote the 2015 release of *Star Wars: The Force Awakens*. Even at the height of his success, though, he was looking ahead to see what else he could do.

"That's the thing: once you've crushed something, you've got to keep moving on. Who knows how long Snapchat's going to be around? Let's crush it again."

While still going strong on Snapchat, Shaun started developing his YouTube channel. Originally he was documenting the scene behind the scenes of his crazy Snapchat adventures and travels, but as he started creating more branded YouTube videos and his life became increasingly packed with meetings, the channel increasingly featured all the characters in his life, from the employees working in the "Spacestation"—Shaun's studio and office—to his wife, Jenny, and his baby girl, Adley. In late 2016, they launched a second YouTube channel, on which they all have free rein to bring their "weird ideas" to life. Shaun envisions it as a sitcom in which all of his friends and family play a distinct role. His hope is that his audience will get addicted to the personalities and story lines just as they once did with shows like *Seinfeld*.

Though his YouTube brand deals today outnumber

those he does for Snapchat, his Snapchat following re-mains robust. In addition, he continues to accept speak-ing engagements, including a TED Talk. He is also working as a consultant helping brands to strategize, work with influencers, and put together strong social-media cam-paigns. In 2017, he announced that he'll be creating branded content for Viacom, including Nickelodeon and MTV. And he recently launched a successful eSports orga-nization with some of the number-one teams in the world. There's no sign of stopping. Every day, this long-haired skater dude with the instincts of a hardened businessman commits to spreading positive messages and giving peo-ple a reason to laugh and have fun.

What's the secret to his success? "Personal relation-ships. I think a lot of people establish fake, one-way relationships—they just want to ask for something, or they want to do a collab and get a shout-out. They don't de-velop those real relationships and provide value and just give, give, give. If you do that, eventually you'll get back, and that's where the success comes."

I have watched this man execute relentlessly for the last five years or so. What I love most about him is how his happiness comes through in everything that he does. He's a classic storyteller who isn't afraid to try anything. While many people find every reason in the world to say no, Shaun says yes. That's his secret sauce.

TWITTER

If the following information sounds a little familiar, as though you might have read it before in *Crush It!*, that's because you did. The strategy for building a brand on Twitter has changed little in nine years, but most people *still* haven't learned how to do it correctly and effectively.

Twitter is the water cooler of society, that place where everyone goes to get the latest update on whatever news or pop-culture event is occurring. The only difference is that, while office workers used to have to wait until the day after an event to gather around and share their knowledge and opinions, now that conversation is happening in real time, 24/7.

At the time of this writing, Twitter, in this one man's opinion, is in a really tricky spot. It continues to remain the only pure social network, a place where people interact with content, with each other, and with events in a way that doesn't happen anywhere else. Other platforms started out as social networks, to be sure, but eventually became content management systems. There is engagement, but on a far smaller scale than on Twitter. On Twitter, in an instant you can dive into any conversation about any topic—cooking, outer space, wine, sneakers, politics, skateboards, seltzer. Done wisely, this engagement will compel people to seek out your content elsewhere. Unfortunately, this ease of interaction led Twitter to develop more into a conversation platform than a consumption platform. People talk a lot on Twitter, and the sheer volume is problematic. You're going to consume a lot more of what I say if you hear me speak at a keynote than if we're having a conversation, because when we talk, especially in a group, we'll probably interrupt each other, talk over each other, and get distracted by what else is going on in the room. It's difficult for consumers to absorb everything you want them to when you're talking to them on Twitter. The constant chatter and massive volume has been great for the spread of ideas, which is good for influencers and media outlets, but the chat glut has also made it harder for people to break out as Twitter personalities.

Twitter 101

Twitter is disproportionately the place to listen, react, and hijack. Problem is, most people aren't very good listeners, and it's often an especially big challenge for the types of people who want to build personal brands so the world will listen to *them*. But listening well is the key to engaging well on Twitter. It's by listening that you can find the conversation threads that can lead you to the people passionate about the subject around which you're going to grow your influence. If you're a lawyer who wants to be the next influential sportscaster, it's likely you're going to put out amazing sports-related commentary on YouTube and create a sports podcast. Getting anyone to give you even a passing glance on those platforms, however, will depend almost exclusively on the quality of your content, and even then a huge number of people just won't see you. But on Twitter, a rising sportscaster could make it her mission to find all the people—every single one—talking about Kolten Wong, Adam Wainwright, the Cardinals, or the Cardinals' archrivals, the Cubs, Chicago, or Wrigley Field, and reply in some unthreatening, interesting way that creates a connection between her and each sports fan. The next day, she could do the very same thing for people talking about the Jets and all Jets-related topics. If she does it well and frequently enough, eventually she can virtually grab these people by the shoulders and point them straight toward her website, YouTube channel, or podcast.

The thing is, it will take a shitload of discipline and patience. Let me define discipline: it's backing up your ambitions with your actions. This rookie will need to spend four, five, even six hours a day on this kind of engagement, often in the predawn hours, if she wants to become the next Linda Cohn. If she just wants a little name recognition from her town's bar regulars when they talk about their local team, then twenty or forty minutes per day will be perfectly adequate. Maybe.

Now, keeping people's attention and nabbing a subscription or a loyal fan will still rely entirely on the quality of what those consumers find on our rookie sportscaster's website, but the point is that Twitter gives you a chance to both lure and lasso—or jab and right hook—people into your orbit in a way that no other platform does. It's a slow, slow, slow process and an immense amount of work, but if you're willing to do it and your content is special, you should see a payoff.

Twitter 201

Biz-dev. Everyone knows that Twitter is still the number-one place to get my attention because, to this day, I'm still consuming what people are saying about me there more than on all other platforms combined. That's true for many other people in different fields. Because it was built to be a conversation platform, Twitter is an interesting place to jump-start biz-dev opportunities or collaborations as you grow your brand—maybe even the best place. For example, some influencers have hundreds of thousands, even millions, of followers on Instagram, but only a few thousand on Twitter. Where do you think they get the most requests for favors or collabs? Instagram. So even though they probably spend more time on Instagram, you're more likely to have a better chance of getting a response if you DM them on Twitter, where there is less competition for their attention.

There are several other advantages to using Twitter as your pillar content:

▶ It's a complete and trustworthy directory. The platform has been around long enough to have perfected its verification system, which gives it a better search function. You can still spend a lot of time guessing whether the Instagram account you're targeting is real or not.

▶ Its retweet feature offers a remarkable opportunity to create instant awareness. Let's say you make a YouTube mash-up of the rapper Logic's music videos. It's unlikely he's going to see it, even if he's tagged. Share the mash-up on Twitter, however, and the retweets can propel your video to dramatic virality, the kind that even the biggest influencers notice. This kind of word of mouth does not exist on Instagram or Snapchat and is enormously beneficial to content creators.

▶ Not only that, you can try to spark that word of mouth many, many more times on Twitter than on other platforms. I post three, maybe four times per day on Instagram, but there are days when I could post forty-seven times on Twitter. The fact that it's as welcoming to the written word as to pictures gives content creators the flexibility and leeway to increase the volume of their storytelling.

On Twitter, you are always just one comment away from getting noticed and making a name for yourself, so the more times you get a chance to talk, the better. Remember, though, that the best dinner guests are not just great storytellers, but also great listeners. So bring all your smarts, your wit, and your cleverness to the party, keep the conversation going by engaging everyone around you, and watch your influence grow and your opportunities multiply. There's no other platform that gives you this opening to introduce yourself to so many people so often. Don't ignore it.

Imagine This

Let's say you're a twenty-two-year-old college student named Anna, and your dream is to be a sports commentator. I know there are a lot of you out there because you e-mail me pretty much every month asking me to help you get an internship at ESPN or *Bleacher Report* or *Barstool Sports*. You know what that means? That means that even the kids who have spent most of their lives steeped in social media and can hardly remember a time before Twitter are still looking at the world through a narrow lens and completely missing the big career and personal brand–building opportunities right in front of them.

The wonderful thing about sports is that they're a great equalizer. Any basketball fan can walk up to a group of twenty people they don't know debating LeBron versus Jordan and within minutes be part of the mix. For many people, they're the easiest icebreaker. Sports also help people ease into new relationships, offering a way to connect with strangers without having to rely on other social identifiers, like your job, neighborhood, or school. Twitter was built for those kinds of conversations. In fact, there's no better place than Twitter for sports personalities and enthusiasts, because there is literally no limit to the number and kind of sports conversations in which you could engage.

Now think about this: who do you think has a better chance of getting an internship with ESPN: (a) the unknown kid who sends her résumé in along with four thousand other people applying for the same job and has nothing but a prayer that the director of the internship program will bother to look at her portfolio, or (b) the kid who becomes a regular, active presence in the Twitter feeds of all the ESPN personalities and staff who actually rely on intern help?

The thing that differentiates sportscasters from one another is their greater or lesser ability to synthesize data, of course, but also the particular ways they add their two or three or nine cents to the event at hand, whether it's the McGregor versus Mayweather fight, or the Cavaliers versus the Warriors, or the Wimbledon tennis finals. Twitter is unmatched in its ability to help you amplify your voice and your brand. If you're looking for a job or hoping to make your mark in an industry, consider your activity there as the longest interview of your life. And that's a good thing. There are few feelings more frustrating than leaving an interview wishing you could have said one more thing to show off what you know or to emphasize your value to an organization. You never have to feel that way on Twitter; the forum gives you endless opportunities to prove why you're special and deserve to be respected.

So use Twitter to show the world—and in particular, all the important people at various sports outlets who might need interns—your unique perspective and personality.

Start by looking at the trending topics (in the mobile app, you'll see them listed when you click on the Search symbol). There is bound to be something sports related there. Click on it, and then start expressing your thoughts. You can do this in two ways. You could just start writing. With a 280-character limit, it could take you eleven tweets to say everything you want to, but that's OK. Or you could try recording a video of yourself talking about the topic (the current video time limit on Twitter is 140 seconds), then posting that. Include the relevant hashtag so that everyone else searching for information on that topic will see your tweets. Once you've exhausted yourself with the trends, start searching other sports topics and inserting yourself into the conversations happening around them by replying to people's tweets. You show you're well rounded by sharing your thoughts all day, every day, via text or video, on everything from the NHL to MMA, the PGA, and World Taekwondo (which was known as the WTF until June 2017, when it rebranded and dropped the word *Fed-*

eration from its name). You reply to famous people, you create content in response to well-known sportswriters, personalities, coaches, and athletes. You give yourself every possible opportunity to be discovered as people hit those hashtags and watch those conversations.

Done right, this should take you four to six hours.

That's day one.

On day two, you do it again—for four to six hours, or as many as you can spare when you're not at work or school. Remember, eleven minutes is eleven more than zero, but also remember, twelve minutes gives you more at bats to win than eleven.

Day three is a Saturday. Awesome! It's your day off! That means you can spend ten to seventeen hours seeking out sports-related topics and engaging with others interested in them, too.

Day four, Sunday, the day of rest. You "sleep in"—an extra hour—so you only get ten to sixteen hours to work, but you make them count.

Day five. Monday. Go to work, go to school. Tweet during any downtime, such as lunch or walking between classes. Meet your parents for dinner (put the phone away). Go home. Study for your upcoming test if you must,* and tweet until two a.m.

Do this repeatedly, consistently, constantly, until your thumbs are callused and your eyes are bleeding, or at least until you feel they should be.

One of those tweets, maybe within those five days but probably more like a year down the line, will be the piece of content that catches the eye of someone at a sports station in Kansas City or Montreal or Chicago, who will reach out to you to find out where you're working and whether you'd be interested in joining their team. Or maybe a news station will contact you and ask you to comment for an article (news stations monitor Twitter closely for material). One piece

---

* Many sports internships are going to require that applicants be enrolled in a degree program or be a recent graduate of one, so in this case, make your tuition worthwhile and do your best.

of content in a Twitter environment can be worth a hundred on any other platform. It's that disproportionately impactful.

I want to make something very clear. This book, like 99 percent of my content, is for people who aren't 100 percent happy, for those who complain or wish or hope or wonder "What if?" I talk about working twelve-, fourteen-, or seventeen-hour days because that's what it took most of today's success stories and entrepreneurial role models to get to where they are. I don't actually recommend unhealthy lifestyles, like getting too little sleep or isolating yourself from your family, but to all the critics who say entrepreneurs like you and me don't have work-life balance or are shortchanging our health, I ask you this: has it ever occurred to you that the people you're insisting should get eight hours of sleep are so unhappy with the sixteen hours they're awake that they're willing to invest this many hours to change their lives for the better? Which would you rather have, a long night's sleep and sixteen hours of misery every day or a little less sleep but twenty hours of wide-awake joy? I'll pick joy every time, and so will most people who are crushing it.

HOW I'M CRUSHING IT

Jared Polin, FroKnowsPhoto

YOUTUBE: FROKNOWSPHOTO

Jared Polin's father had a great way of explaining why he always wanted to be his own boss: "I'm not going to be told when I can take a leak." A children's clothing sales-man, he was known for his honesty. When Jared decided to go into business for himself, he vowed that honesty would be one of his calling cards, too. Along with his hair pick.

Jared uses a hair pick as a business card because he has a seriously big afro, and because he is the founder of FroKnowsPhoto, a YouTube channel dedicated to "fun and informative videos" about everything you'd want to know about photography, from proper lighting techniques to choosing the best gear. He spent his youth working in a camera store, started shooting professionally at the age of fifteen, and spent ten years touring with bands. This is not someone who ever had to think hard to identify his passion.

For years he had had a beautiful website that featured his best work, but he hadn't seen much business come of it. He was twenty-nine years old. His mother had passed away unexpectedly of cancer, and he'd stayed home to help his father take care of his centenarian grandmother. He was shooting weddings, the usual gigs photographers do to make their living, and earning $20K, maybe $30K a year. At the time, most people were saying that blogs were the way to build an audience, but he didn't consider himself a writer. Yet he'd watch other photographers' YouTube channels and be consistently unimpressed with the information they were putting out. Rather than criticize and tell them what they were doing wrong in their comments sections, he simply decided to do it better.

He'd attended an event, bartering his photography skills for a ticket, where he had heard this loud wine salesman talk about how he had used video to grow his family's liquor store.

This guy was very real and not trying to sell anything, even though he'd just written a book. And he said, "There's no secret to being successful on the Internet. You need to be good at what you do; you need to be passionate about it and go crush it." That resonated with me. It was like a weight lifted off my shoulders because someone else was saying what I was thinking. I had tried some things in the past, to make a couple videos and put them up, but for whatever reason, my head wasn't in it. I just wasn't ready, I guess, at the time. And reading the book, something clicked, and I thought, *Now I'm ready to do this*. He did this in the wine world; there's no reason why I can't go out there and exploit it in the photo world.

The original purpose of the videos Jared made was to help him book more photo gigs. Instead, people started coming to him for advice about how to buy camera equipment. Previously he'd always considered anyone else taking pictures as the competition. The last thing he'd consider doing was helping them so they could compete for the jobs he wanted. Now he did a one-eighty and decided he was going to give all his information away for free. "Because you know what? People don't have what I have."

There was another motivation as well. His mother's death lay heavily on him. For years she had asked her son to teach her how to better use a camera, but time had gotten away from them until they didn't have any left. "It's one of the biggest regrets in my life. She wanted to learn photography. There's no reason I shouldn't have taken the time to do this. Other people need to benefit from the knowledge that I have so they can be successful and continue on."

He maxed out a $15,000 credit card with an 18-month period of 0 percent financing, which he suspects was meant for his father but had his name on it. He bought camera equipment and merch, then started putting out content.

I found the thing that I could do, and I beat the shit out of it. I locked myself away for two years. Every day, day in and day out. I shot a video every single day. Wake up in the morning, come up with an idea, shoot a video, edit it, have lunch, come back, put it out into the world, have dinner, then stay up until one or two in the morning replying to comments. I didn't use tele-prompters or anything. If I made a mistake, I would make fun of myself and keep going, partly because I didn't know how to edit video. All I knew how to do was put a beginning and an end on it. Sometimes good enough is good enough.

Within six months, he saw a rise in viewership: one hundred views, then two hundred. All along, he was com-menting, answering questions, and interacting with view-ers. He made himself available to anyone who wanted to talk.

Crush It! talks about building your business off of search.twitter.com. I also made it a point to answer every single e-mail that came in. I put up my Skype number so that anybody could call at any hour. If I was sitting there, I would take the call. Then I would get the caller's permission to record the call, because there's nothing like free content. They were asking me ques-tions, and if they're asking it, then other people prob-ably have the same one.

He made some connections to appear on other people's YouTube channels. As the number of viewers started to climb, so did the number of subscribers. In short order, Nikon and Canon and other photography brands started asking him to review gear. Sometimes they even offered to pay him to do it. "I'm very up front. Someone might pay me, but they can't tell me what to say. If there's going to be something bad about a product, I'm telling you what's bad, whether they're paying me or not. It's all about building credibility."

The free model worked so well that in the end he didn't need to take other people's photography jobs. Now he barters trades with bands and musicians he wants to cover. They give him access, and he gets more content to share with the world. In seven years, he's put out 2,400 videos, all dedicated to helping other people become better photographers, and received one hundred million views on YouTube. At the end of the first two years, he'd generated about $80,000 in revenue. Today he says he can generate seven figures.

> You are not going to be successful unless you put the work in. If anybody tells you otherwise, they're full of shit. It's all of the perseverance and all of the hard work you put in in the decades leading up to it that make you ready. Are you passionate about what you're doing? Are you good at what you're doing? Then fucking do it. It's one thing to read the book; it's another thing to take action.

I've watched Jared carefully for years, and what stands out to me is his inability to complain. Like me, he put out

hundreds of hours of content while receiving little traction up front. But that didn't stop him. That's the difference between him and almost everyone else, including
most of the people who will read this book—he didn't give
up too early. Persistence is everything.

YOUTUBE

YouTube makes me so happy. It's here that I believe I can possibly help change a life faster than anywhere else. Since 2009, millions of people have quit their jobs and started making a living on this platform. It's the whole reason *Crush It!* and this book and the books in between and everything else in my professional world came to be.

Ironically, YouTube is also where I made one of the biggest mistakes in my career. I was a breakout star on YouTube in 2006, but by the time I started writing *Crush It!*, I had decided that Viddler, its competitor, had a tagging system and management team that made it a superior platform for me and my content, which was unusually long by 2007 standards. In addition, I'll admit I was swayed by a short-term economic decision: the company gave me substantial equity in the business.* I was certain that my advocacy and ability to put the platform in context for everyone would ensure its rise to prominence,

---

* See? When I tell you that it's not worth sacrificing long-term success for short-term economic gain, I speak from experience. When I finally got around to building up my YouTube presence around 2015, I had only about forty thousand subscribers. Imagine how many millions more people I could have reached during all that time if I hadn't had my head turned by Viddler's lucrative offer.

but I was wrong. But you know what? It didn't matter, because in the end, whether I was talking Viddler, YouTube, or Google Video, my advice on how to crush it in video would have been 100 percent the same.

I suspect YouTube has created more wealth and more opportunities in the *Crush It!* model than any other platform to date. It's certainly the most important platform for building a personal brand, though Instagram is closing the gap quickly. It could take the place of television. Increasing numbers of people are streaming YouTube onto their TV screens, and during prime-time hours on an average day in the United States, more eighteen-to-forty-nine-year-olds visit YouTube than any TV network, even on mobile alone. That's tough news. I know that not everybody who's reading this book is cut out for video, which is why I'm so thankful that other alternatives exist to beautifully showcase the written word, still images, and audio. However, let's be real. With perhaps the notable exception of J. K. Rowling, author of the Harry Potter series, and a handful of other writers, in general over the last thirty years, video stars have financially outperformed stars in every other medium.

YouTube 101

Please, even if you don't think you're video material, give the platform a try. So many people don't think of themselves as cameraworthy, but vlogging and documenting doesn't demand that you be glamorous or beautiful or really superficially special at all. Have you looked at what's out there? Aside from the beauty bloggers, the bodybuilders, and the rising pop idols—in other words, aside from everyone in an industry where your looks *really* matter—everyone on YouTube looks pretty damned ordinary. There are vloggers with disfiguring tumors, vloggers with disabilities, vloggers of all ages and shapes. Vlogging is a terrific way to document instead of create, which means that literally anyone can do it. You don't need to be accomplished (at least not in the way 99 percent of you reading this define accomplishment) to break out on this platform because, remember, when you're documenting and not creating, you're allowed to learn as you go. You don't have to be an expert (yet). You don't have to be successful (yet). The only thing you really do have to do is make the road to getting there interesting.

Now, interesting is subjective. You know what I find super interesting to watch? Videos about hitting up garage sales. And I'm not the only one. As I write, a quick search on YouTube shows videos devoted to the topic of garage saling receiving as many as 50,000, 99,000, and 137,000 views. Don't ever decide for yourself that videos about you or the things you like to do won't be compelling to anyone else. Let the market decide. Trust me, it'll be honest with you.

Vlogging is a great equalizer, and YouTube is the vlogging mother ship. It's the platform where the person no one thought would amount to anything can make it. It's a tool for finding your best angle, and I don't mean camera angle. If you have a lot of interests, if you aren't sure where your greatest skills lie, if you wonder whether you have the kind of charisma and appeal that draws audiences to YouTube personalities, or if you simply can't decide whether you'd rather be the number-one American authority on pajamas or the go-to guru for kombucha, pick up your phone and start documenting your day. Put the results up daily as a YouTube vlog. See which posts get the most attention and double down on whatever it is that's making those posts stick. But you have to put something out to know if you've got the goods. I didn't mull over whether I should start Wine Library or debate whether I was good enough to deserve a YouTube audience. The second I thought filming a wine review show was a good idea, I had an employee go to Best Buy to buy the camera, filmed the first episode, and posted it. That first episode looks and sounds totally different from the ones I created even four months later because I figured out that I could be me. I'd held back, not because I was worried about the opinion of the world at large, but because I was afraid if I really let loose, I'd jeopardize all the hard-won relationships the wine store had with longtime customers who bought $10,000 of wine from me every month.

If you look at the first episode, I'm almost unrecognizable. Not because I'm over a decade younger and fifteen pounds heavier, but because my personality is so subdued. I say very wine-expert things like, "When I smell this, it reminds me of a classic Clinet or a VCC" and "I'm not going to push the Pétrus . . ." Then in episode 11, you can see on the wall behind me a framed black-and-white photo of Muhammad Ali and Joe Frazier battling it out in the 1971 Fight of the Century. That may have been the first piece of the real me, the boxing-loving me, that made its way into the show.

In episode 40, I start talking about joy and passion and cut to a clip from the televised 2006 NFL draft, where I was caught on camera screaming my head off with excitement with my friends and my brother, A. J., in response to the announcement that the Jets had selected D'Brickashaw Ferguson, an offensive tackle from the University of Virginia, over quarterback Matt Leinart. I was starting to reveal other sides of me, because, as I said at the end of the episode, "You've got to be passionate about other things besides wine." It's right around this time that I started to realize that the world was changing so much that this channel could potentially get much bigger than I'd ever anticipated, and it might be worth risking a few short-term wine losses in exchange for the long-term value of allowing myself to be me.

By episode 57, I give a virtual finger to the establishment. Episode 58 gets even more real with the title, "I'm Not Pissed," and reveals that I turned down two network opportunities, one in a travel genre, one in a food-and-wine genre, because I didn't believe that TV was the future. Now remember, this is supposed to be a wine show! My energy is rising, my voice is going faster, and I'm being more direct. And then my confidence really kicks in with comments like, "We're the best marketers in the wine business. We don't need a blog to sell wine." I start dropping colorful phrases like "bull crap" and "Taste the goddamn wine!" like bright pomegranate seeds into my monologues. By episode 61, when I start asking for people to keep e-mailing me because my mail was confirming that I was hitting a nerve and getting people excited and interested, my opening is less *Masterpiece Theatre*, more WWE.

As you can see, the delivery, quality, and content of Wine Library TV changed over time. I gave the show time to evolve. I gave myself time to get comfortable and relax into the format. I gave myself time to get to know my audience and listen to what it was saying. It has been pointed out to me that my first video was ten times better than some people's hundredth in terms of quality and content. Maybe, but again, quality is subjective; some people are successful despite being complete idiots because the public loves to watch them be idiots. For sure I'm coherent and you can tell I know my shit. That was definitely a good start, but remember, there is no way I could have known that I'd be good on video at the time. If I had sat on my idea of starting a wine show and worried and second-guessed myself, I could have probably found a hundred reasons not to do it. Thank God I didn't stop to do any of that but went with my gut. YouTube isn't going to make you charismatic and interesting, but it will expose you if you are. It can't do that, however, if you don't put yourself out there. Give yourself a year to adjust and try different approaches and see what kind of response you get. Listen to your audience. Ultimately, it all boils down to this: don't let perfection be your enemy. Do not be another dreamer who puts up ten episodes, gets trolled or ignored, gets discouraged, and takes the channel down. For God's sake, give yourself a fair chance to succeed.

Every single thing that has ever happened on television can happen on YouTube. You can break out as a pop star. You can be a filmmaker. You can become Billy Mays, the infomercial pitchman. You want to become a morning TV star? Start a morning TV show on YouTube. You want to be the next Dr. Drew? Start a Q&A show. You want to be the next Rachael Ray, Oprah, Tavis Smiley, or Chris Hardwick?

Then start cooking, mentoring, interviewing, or talking pop culture on YouTube. Tomorrow.

Yes, it will be harder today than it would have been had you started doing this in 2011, when there were a lot of people watching but not as many creating, but if you are really talented, smart, funny, or creative, you will win. It might take you a few more months or even years than it would have in 2011, but it will happen.

Taking the "document, don't create" approach means you are conceivably going to pour a shitload of boring content into the miasma of boring content already living on YouTube.

That's OK.

You know why?

Because if in the end the rest of the world agrees that your content is boring, you'll know that you're not cut out for this, and you can move on to something else.

Or it might be because you'll get an e-mail from one of the six people who watched episode 94 of your 200 yarn episodes, who happens to be the CEO of your favorite yarn company, telling you he'd love to work together one day if you're interested. You decide you're never going to become a PBS star, call him up, and work out a deal where you create educational videos for the company website. They're a big company, so they get four hundred thousand views per episode, allowing you to build your brand through them. They're also big enough to pay you very well to do something you love.

It might be because you discover that, even though the general public didn't get caught up in your craft-beer vlog, you had more fun doing that than you've ever had in your career as a software developer. So you approach Yuengling about making educational training videos for their staff, and they bring you on board for a high five-figure salary. The pay isn't that different from what you earned before, but you go to bed happy every Sunday, excited to get back to work the next day.

Did you become a millionaire? No. But only a tiny percent of the people who try this will. That's irrelevant. The point is to dream big and then make the practical adjustments necessary once you see where your potential lies. However, you will never, ever know the extent of that potential until you try. I guarantee it's greater than you think it is.

For a couple of years now, the tech-savvy early adopters have been watching YouTube on their television sets. Very soon, everyone is going to be doing it, and the next generation will not see any difference between the two. YouTube will be television; television will be YouTube. YouTube is a monster. Yet Facebook is making plans to add more features that will make it look a lot like YouTube. With YouTube in possession of a decade of equity as the established video platform, Facebook is going to have to work its ass off to compete. As you're about to see, it's gonna be a hell of a fight.

Imagine This

Let's say your name is Sam. You're a fifty-two-year-old insurance salesperson in Alabama. Your twins just headed off to college, leaving you alone with your partner and the two dogs who have been a part of the family since the children were tiny. As excited as you are to start this new chapter in your life, you know it's going to be hard adjusting to a home where there are no longer any kids around to make messes, cause drama, and add sparks and unpredictability to an otherwise staid and calm life. You've been working for the same insurance company for twenty-two years. You think retirement is probably only about ten to fifteen years away. You've saved steadily and invested wisely, you have little debt, and the house is mostly paid off. Life is fine.

Just fine.

Then your best friend sends you a video called "6 Mins for the Next 60 Years of Your Life." (Google it.)

You realize that you have potentially thirty to forty more years ahead of you, and you want them to be more than just fine. You want them to be great. And with the kids finding their independence, you now have about twice the number of hours you once did to make them that way.

You start thinking about all the fun hobbies and interests you let drop as life became busier and your responsibilities increased. You always loved to dance. Your mom forced you into ballroom dance classes when you were a child, and to your surprise you not only really enjoyed the rhythms and moves of salsa, merengue, and swing, but you were damn good at them. The skill served you well on the dating scene—it's how you met your spouse. But you both let the hobby drop as you settled into married life. It's also been six years since you set foot in a gym; by now your knees would probably buckle after two rock steps.

But maybe they wouldn't? And if they did, maybe instead of pathetic, that could be . . . funny? Maybe it would be something you and your partner could laugh about together?

You make a pitch to your partner: let's get in shape and start dancing again. And to keep us accountable, let's film the whole process. Your partner sees how excited you are about this, gingerly pinches the roll of fat that has settled around their waist, and agrees.

You discover that yes, your YMCA membership card does still work even though you haven't set foot in the place for six years. That first day on the treadmill goes pretty well, and you're feeling so optimistic, you hit the weights, too. It makes for a triumphant first three-minute video. Unfortunately, your muscles revolt against the unusual physical activity by seizing up on you so badly that you're laid out flat on your back for the next two days. You film your next two videos from your bed, filling in your *two fans* with information about yourself, your feelings about dance, and why you're embarking on this project. Those two fans are your kids, by the way. Whatever.

You change your eating habits, you commit to the gym, and you start attending dance lessons twice a week. Every day, you film a vlog post, sharing what you're liking, what you're not, your diet tips, what you learned in class, and anything else you think might be of interest to your viewers. After a month, you have four subscribers. You're pretty sure the two new ones are your kids' roommates. Whatever.

For six months, you and your spouse continue on this journey of self-improvement, and the results are amazing. Between the two of you, you've lost twelve pounds, and the shared experience of learning new things together has rekindled a spark that had faded in your marriage. You're having tons of fun, and it shows in your videos. You don't know who all those subscribers are now, but while talking to those who comment, you've figured out that at least a handful are older relatives of the students sharing your kids' dorms.

You eventually find the courage to sign up at the newcomer level in a local dance competition, and while you don't place at the top, you don't feel that you've embarrassed yourself, either. Episode 489 shows you driving six hours to attend a statewide competition, where you take home the Beginner bronze. Ensuing videos document your journey to Championship competitions, as well as the transformation of your marriage from ho-hum to hot stuff.

Things continue to get better. Over the course of two years of training and vlogging, you pick up the attention of thousands of people who are inspired by your commitment to later-in-life fitness and a beautiful art form normally associated with the young and svelte. You and your spouse are anything but, but people love watching you anyway. Your fans help you pick out costumes, make workout suggestions, and trade dance stories, but you find they're just as eager to talk about strategies they've used to reinvigorate their personal relationships as they are about your hobby. As your audience has grown, you've gotten to meet some of your fans, and you're stunned at how pleased they are to meet you in person, how they want to pose for pictures with you as if you're some kind of television star. Your following gets big enough that you think it's worth reaching out to other

YouTube dance channels and asking if they'd be interested in submitting some content to your page or doing an interview. Dance schools, dance teachers, fan pages for *So You Think You Can Dance* and *Dancing with the Stars*, and dance-gear brands, dance conferences, and competitions start reaching out to ask if they can post their brands or make appearances on your show. You start getting sponsorship offers from workout-gear companies, theaters, and sports drinks. By day, you sell insurance. In the predawn hours and late at night, you engage and biz-dev while your partner edits video. On the weekends, you dance. Together, you're having the time of your lives.

It's been six years since you started this project, Sam. You're now fifty-eight years old, and your income has nearly doubled now that it's subsidized by brands associated with dance, healthy lifestyles, and personal development. You think you'll be able to retire from your insurance job in a year or two, after you've earned enough to pay off the kids' school debt. You have no intention of ever retiring from your vlog, though, even though it takes a lot of work to keep up the momentum. Nothing about this transformation has been easy, but it's been incredible fun.

I made this story up, but it's not fantasy. You can do it, or your parents can. Hell, your grandparents can. It's a scenario that could be replicated in real life. In fact, it's already been done.

YouTube Best Practices

If you want to increase the amount of time people spend watching every video you post on your channel as a whole, make sure you can answer the questions below.

VIDEO OPTIMIZATION

TITLES: How much thought have you put into your video title? Does the title accurately reflect the video's content? Is the majority of the title viewable on mobile? Is the title short and concise, emotionally driven, and/or keyword optimized?

DESCRIPTIONS: Are the top two lines of the description keyword optimized? Are there links to other similar videos or playlists in the description? Is there a subscribe link? Are there links to your other social-media accounts? Are all of the links clickable and trackable?

TAGS: Are there at least ten tags in the description? Are both one-word and phrase tags included? Do the tags accurately reflect the video's content? Are the tags valuable, that is, do they have high search volumes but low competition? You can find this out by using tools like VidIQ, Google Adwords Keyword Planner, and Keywordtool.io.

THUMBNAILS: Does the thumbnail accurately reflect the video's content? If there is text on the thumbnail, is it easy to read on all devices? If there is text, does it complement the title?

YOUTUBE CARDS: To extend watch time on your channel, are you including YouTube cards within your video to drive traffic to other relevant videos you've posted?

CHANNEL OPTIMIZATION

BANNER: Does the banner accurately reflect the channel's content and genre? Does the graphic transfer well to all devices?

ABOUT SECTION/CHANNEL DESCRIPTION: Are the top two lines keyword optimized? Is the first paragraph an overview of the channel? Have you included the upload schedule? Are all of the social-media links clickable? (They don't have to be trackable.)

PLAYLISTS: Does the channel have custom playlists? Do the playlists have keyword-optimized descriptions? Are the playlists featured on the landing page of the channel?

CHANNEL TRAILER: Is a channel trailer displayed on the landing page? Does the channel trailer accurately reflect the channel's content and genre? Is the channel trailer telling the best story in the shortest amount of time?

HOW I'M CRUSHING IT

Daniel Markham, What's Inside?

IG: @WHATSINSIDE

It's fitting that a science project was responsible for shifting Daniel Markham's career from pharmaceutical sales rep to half of a world-traveling father-son duo devoted to cutting things in two. Decades of testing, experimentation, and life experience led to his and his son's "overnight success."

Growing up, Dan had always wanted to be an entrepreneur, but upon graduating from college with a young family, he applied his degree in global business and finance to a position as a pharmaceutical sales rep. The money was good, but for years he put up websites and dabbled in side hustles, or, in his words, "little random small businesses that totally failed," in the hopes that one would take off and allow him to leave his steady job. When YouTube came along, he put up videos of his kids and wife to share with the rest of his family, who didn't live near him in Utah. He'd always monetized his websites with Google AdSense, throwing up little pop-up ads, and he did the same for the YouTube videos even though he'd never made any money this way. No one was watching.

One day his son, Lincoln, came to him for help with

his second-grade science project. The assignment: to ask and answer a question of his own choosing. The year before, he'd asked, "Why do we have boogers?" and had stuck a giant nose stuffed with green goo on his poster-board presentation. This year he was interested in finding out why humans have earwax, but Dan felt that was too similar. So after thinking about it, Lincoln decided that since he loved sports, he'd like to find out what was inside a sports ball. With his father's help, he started cutting balls in half and putting together his project. Dan decided to film the process, posting the results on one of his YouTube channels that he renamed Lincoln Markham to make it easy to identify. The idea was that after making his presentation, Lincoln could share the name of the channel with his teacher and classmates, and they could go watch it on their own time. Dan had already monetized about eighty videos by then, including the previous year's booger video, playing around with the titles and tag words to make them more appealing, He added this one to the lot. It was January 2014.

Almost a year later, on a winter day in December 2014, Dan got an AdSense notification that he'd earned four dollars. He checked his analytics. It hadn't come from his websites. He checked YouTube. Someone was watching, enough someones to generate income. Inexplicably, YouTube had decided it liked his video and had started suggesting it when people were watching videos about baseball. People were clicking on it, and some were commenting, offering suggestions for other types of balls Lincoln could cut open. "Maybe this is it," Dan thought. He showed Lincoln what was happening and asked him if he was interested in doing some more videos. Together, they decided to go all in.

They hid the other videos on the channel, changed the name to What's Inside? and started cutting. They'd spend four or five hours together every Saturday, using Dan's phone to film videos of themselves cutting open various types of balls, and Dan would throw them up to the platform. As they learned more about how the You-Tube algorithm worked, they continued to film on Satur-days, even when they were traveling, but they released only one video per week. The videos got better and more polished as Dan taught himself to use Final Cut Pro and enhanced the storytelling elements of the videos. For example, when they cut up a football, they opened with footage of themselves throwing a football around. They learned even more by attending video conferences and networking with other YouTubers. It was at one of these events, the first CVX Live, that Dan heard adventure-and-extreme-sports videographer Devin Graham, aka devin-supertramp, announce that the way he made money on YouTube was 10 percent from AdSense, 20 percent from licensing content, and 70 percent from sponsored vid-eos. "It just completely blew my mind. I was like, 'Oh, my gosh, you can make money from brands that would wanna put their stuff on there?' That was new to me."

It was summer 2015, and Dan scored his first brand deal by making a pitch on a website called FameBit, a marketing site where brands post offers to pay creatives to promote their products. He got paid around $250 to cut open a Rubik's Cube, and then $1,000 to cut open a mattress. "I thought we had it made. A thousand dollars, and we're just cutting open a mattress!"

A few months later, he met Shaun "Shonduras" McBride (see page 167), who told him that with their channel's reach—they now had almost one million subscribers—they should be pitching the advertising agencies that run big influencer marketing campaigns. "Back to the hustle. I had my day job where I was selling drugs and I was traveling to eight different states. And I would sit there at night in hotels looking up the people who spoke at VidCon, the biggest video conference in the country. Anybody who looked like they were from an advertising agency, I would Google them and find out what company they worked for, and reach out, either by e-mail or their Contact Us page."

One of those agencies responded. Dan explained that if they were looking for creative ideas for their brands, he and Lincoln would love to work with them. "'We are family friendly and we cut stuff open. It's like an unboxing channel on steroids.' And they said, 'Well, why don't you sign this NDA and we'll talk.'"

It turned out the agency represented Bill and Melinda Gates. What's Inside? and a few other YouTube channels were chosen to bring attention to their annual letter outlining their position on current global issues and challenging people to work for positive change in the world. The theme of that year's letter was "Two Superpowers We Wish We Had." Dan, who was born in the Philippines, spoke Tagalog, and had served two years there as a missionary for the Church of Jesus Christ of Latter-day Saints (LDS), decided that his superpower would be to bring clean, drinkable water to the developing world. His idea was to bring Lincoln to the Philippines to show him why the lack of potable water was such a serious issue.

This was their first "big brand" deal, and it was an important moment. "We needed to keep hustling and trying to find brands that we liked and that we wanted to work with that would make sense for our channel. We don't want to align ourselves with a brand that we don't support ourselves." This meant turning down deals, sometimes extremely lucrative ones. Dan is proud of Lincoln for talking sense into him when he had his head turned by an advertising agency that offered them something in the $30K-to-$50K range to do a video of them cutting open a toy. There was one problem.

It wasn't super interesting. If we cut it open, people would think, *Why did I watch this?* But honestly, I was going to find a way to do it. I told Lincoln about it. I was a little apprehensive, but it was good money, like a quarter of my annual salary from my day job. And Lincoln said, "No, Dad, absolutely not. We would totally be sellouts if we did that. Our audience would hate it." And as soon as he said it, I was like, "You're totally right." At the time he was ten years old.

They didn't do it. Instead, they posted a different video they were pretty sure would also disappoint their viewers. It was of them cutting open a rattlesnake rattle. They had traveled to the Phoenix Zoo to film the cut as part of the opening about three months earlier, but they'd never posted the video because Dan knew from his research that it would be anticlimactic—there's nothing inside a rattlesnake rattle. But they had no other videos for that week because they'd been on vacation, so they decided to edit the ending for that purpose, even though they were tired from their road trip. It was a Saturday night. Dan spent about seven hours editing and published the video a few minutes before leaving for church the next morning.

That post became the third most viral video on all of YouTube in 2016, racking up forty-two million views in its first seven days. An entire new audience arrived, many of whom were significantly older than the demographic Dan and Lincoln had appealed to before. Among them were people who worked at advertising agencies and brands. Now instead of hustling until three a.m. to find and reach out to big marketing players, the big marketing players were coming to Dan.

He quit his sales job in July 2016.

The generation that's my age, they don't understand social media at all. And then you put in my parents, who are even older. For me to say I'm leaving a really good job that took me a long time to get to where I am, to step away from that to make YouTube videos, they were definitely scared, even when I told them the numbers. Those conversations were hard, because you don't want to feel that you're letting people down or that people are worried about you.

His wife, who had always been supportive but liked her full-time job working for a Fortune 100 company, quit when it became clear that the family balance that was so important to them couldn't be sustained with both parents working such intense hours. And Lincoln? Lincoln still makes videos with his dad, but he also goes to school, plays golf, and hangs with his friends and sisters like any normal boy. Dan is adamant about protecting his son's childhood, and his daughters' now that they're running a family channel, too. He keeps a healthy perspective about the magical ride his family is enjoying.

I want Lincoln to feel like he is still a kid, not like he has a full-time job. I'm looking at a pile of twenty things that would be awesome and timely and good to cut open right now, but I want Lincoln to get home from school and go play with his friends today, so I'm not going to do that. It's a tricky balance.

Nike e-mails and says, "We want Lincoln to be one of the top global influencers for this campaign." Whether or not Lincoln is a top global influencer—and I have a hard time thinking that he is—the fact that Nike thinks he is is something Lincoln has on his résumé that will never go away. I've done a lot of talking about brand deals and hustling to get those brand deals, but at the end of the day, meeting Bill Gates for that first video . . . forget about the money. It will forever go down as something that we've done as a family. This is all stuff that if YouTube went away tomorrow, has been amazing life experiences.

You never know what is going to take off in life. Definitely nothing is going to take off if you are not consistently working hard and trying different things forever. I never thought that I'd be cutting things open, but if I didn't try and fail at all these other things for all those years, this would never have come about.

Dan Markham and his family are practitioners. They did their research, they paid attention to all the little details, and they stayed true to their brand. It's exciting to me to see a family doing so well because they put in the work—and executed.

FACEBOOK

Facebook remains the juggernaut of the social-media game, a platform on par with YouTube for personal brand building and wealth creation. That may come as a surprise to a few readers. Facebook is often thought of as the old-fogy platform, the place where Boomers and Gen Xers share pictures of their families and fill out questionnaires to find out which *GoT* character they most resemble, not the place where the young generation is spending its time and money. That's just not the case. Here's the reality: if you're going to build a personal brand and try to monetize it, you *have* to have a Facebook page. Period. It has almost 2 billion monthly active users, more than half of whom use it daily. There are 1.15 billion daily active users on mobile. If you're crushing it on Snapchat, YouTube, or Instagram but don't have a full-throttle Facebook strategy, you're severely limiting your potential and growth.

Facebook 101

There are a few reasons for this. First, unlike any other platform, Facebook gives you the gift of flexibility. Written content and photographs don't work on YouTube. Instagram allows for a maximum of one-minute videos on a user's main page at the time of this writing. There's no way long written content is getting traction on Snapchat, but on Facebook a thirteen-paragraph blog post will work. You can post pictures, and they'll work. You can embed a SoundCloud audio play, and it will work. A thirteen-second video will work. So will a thirty-one-minute video. Facebook offers complete and utter creative flexibility and has the greatest ad-targeting product ever created. No one is too cool for Facebook. If you haven't already done so, go to Facebook right now and register your fan page, because even if it's not the place where you create the pillar content for your personal brand, it is where everything you do on every other platform will come to live for the remainder of your personal brand's existence.

Facebook is not only a canvas where you can create original content, but also an imperative distribution channel. The DNA of Facebook is word of mouth. It is the place where sharing culture has thrived beyond measure. On other platforms, you generally either hit a grand slam or you strike out. Not so on Facebook. There, with sixty-one shares, you're getting at least a single every day. If you're good at creating content, on another day you could hit a double with two hundred shares. You might drop down to thirteen shares with the next piece of content, only to follow up with something spectacular that gets you seven thousand. With every share, no matter how micro, you're building awareness of your brand in a native way. If anything, it's the best place for people with no followers to begin their personal branding efforts.

Because of its incredibly detailed targeting capabilities—you can specify your audience by their interests, of course, but also by their zip codes or their employers—Facebook is also an incredible place for someone with a small budget. It's an insanely valuable platform when a nobody launching her fashionista brand has to spend only thirteen dollars to boost or target her post of a pretty top and conceivably get as many as 2,600 impressions, depending on her targeting choices. (An "impression" is electronically recorded each time an ad is displayed on a user's screen.) The cost per thousand impressions (CPM, the M standing for *mille*, Latin for "thousand") fluctuates with the market, but right now it is still one of the cheapest yet most effective ad products in existence, comparable to Google Adwords back in the early aughts. That won't always be the case. Eighteen months after this book is published, Facebook ad prices will have doubled or more. Take advantage of this wide-open runway while you still can and jumpstart your brand awareness.

Finally, as big as YouTube is, by the time this book is published, Facebook will be emerging as a fierce competitor in video. Mark Zuckerberg called video a "mega trend" of the same nature as mobile and has made it clear that video is Facebook's future. In 2016, he told *BuzzFeed*, "I wouldn't be surprised if you fast-forward five years and most of the content that people see on Facebook and are sharing on a day-to-day basis is video." When Facebook wants something to work, it puts all its support behind it. The effect on the social-media landscape is generally something like a tectonic plate shift (the platform is in the process of working out deals to produce original content in partnerships with millennial-friendly outlets like Group Nine Media, producer of *The Dodo*, and Vox Media). Knowing that, wouldn't it be foolish to bypass the opportunity to get in early?

You might be thinking, *I already make YouTube videos. I'll just put them on Facebook. Two birds, one stone, done.* Not so fast. Facebook's algorithm will always give preferential treatment to native Facebook content. You'll get far greater reach by creating an original video for Facebook than by recycling something from another platform. Does the video have great copy alongside it? Are the first three seconds captivating? Does it show an understanding of the mind-set of the Facebook demographic that would love to share it with a family member or friend? Does it compel an action right there and then? Video is still something of a novelty on Facebook, which means it has the potential to be noticed faster and get greater engagement than whatever you might post on YouTube.

That doesn't mean you shouldn't post on YouTube or anywhere else, of course, but do not underestimate the power that doubling down on Facebook could have on your brand. Facebook is the first platform that has combined the ability to do marketing, sales, and branding all in one place, and it is still vastly underpriced for the amount of attention you can get there from its nearly two billion monthly users.

Facebook 201

Facebook Live. Facebook has gone all in on Live, trying to give users a place to indulge in the raw, immediate experience of engaging directly with viewers in real time. It's powerful stuff, but be aware that live video is the hardest art form. If you eliminate the news, sports, awards shows, and *Saturday Night Live*, there are very few live TV shows, and for good reason. It takes enormous skill to captivate an audience enough to disrupt their routine at the moment you want their attention. That's a much bigger ask than trying to get people to watch you on their own time. And yet, the spontaneity can really work in your favor. If you can crystallize a special moment and share it with your fans in real time, it can become something truly special to them, too. Just ask Candace Payne of Dallas.

Never heard of her? You might know her better as Chewbacca Mom. On May 19, 2016, Payne opened up Facebook Live to show her Facebook friends a present she bought for herself—a roaring Chewbacca mask. She was so excited, she couldn't even wait to get home; she filmed from inside her car while still sitting in the Kohl's parking lot. She titled the post "It's the Simple Joys in Life." It was a funny look, but what really caught people's attention was her infectious, unstoppable laughter as she delighted in her purchase. Maybe people were feeling jaded; maybe they were weary of heavy content about upcoming elections and other serious topics. For whatever reason, the people who saw the post loved it so much, they started sharing it, and so did everyone else who saw it. With 162 million views as of December 2016, it became the most popular Facebook Live video of that year. As many have pointed out, the vast majority of the people who saw that video viewed it long after it was no longer live, but the live format is what made that moment possible. Had Payne known she was posting for posterity, she might have been more self-conscious. She might have planned in her head what she was going to say. Instead, she just opened up the phone and started filming with her guard down, allowing her personality to shine as bright as two Tatooine suns. You can't get more authentic, and people fell head over heels. For a little while, she was part of the celebrity circuit, appearing on talk shows and being featured in the media. She was rewarded handsomely by Kohl's with thousands of dollars' worth of gift cards and merchandise and she was invited to meet Mark Zuckerberg at Facebook. Hasbro, which made the original Wookie mask, presented her with a custom-made action figure with her head (in a removable mask) attached to a Wookie body. But what's really cool is how Payne used her fifteen minutes of fame to continue building her brand as a positive, deeply religious person dedicated to spreading hope, joy, and optimism. She landed a TLCme video series, and her website revealed a long list of speaking engagements. She signed a multibook deal. Her first book, *Laugh It Up*, published in November 2017, was written, she said in a video she made while preparing to send her manuscript to her editor, "for those of you who think that joy is a frivolous thing that you don't deserve."

Candace Payne's story is the stuff of dreams, the kind of moment that can't be planned. That's why I wouldn't recommend Facebook Live for most people unless they've perfected their video technique and seen success for a few years and are ready to up their game. It's not generally the place to start from zero, because the experience might be a bit like a first-time rider jumping on a bike without training wheels. For those of you who are ready, though, Live could capture a one-in-a-million moment that you never saw coming and put you on the map.* John Lee Dumas, creator of Entrepreneurs on Fire, is a believer, too.

> Without a doubt, Facebook Live is the next thing. I'm having incredible success using platforms like Wirecast and BeLive.tv, which are just tools that allow me to sit at my computer and do a Facebook Live, but they also have text overlay, pull people's comments in, and have full-show interaction. And just the engagement that I'm having, the real time–ness—it's just been a different level.
>
> Everybody's there; they get that little blip notification. "Hey, John's hanging out live right now." I actually call it Tea with JLD just as a cute little rhyme. I pour a cup of tea, I sit on Facebook Live, and I usually go on a rant about some topic for five or ten minutes, and then I start answering questions. Just hanging out—could be thirty minutes, could be an hour—and I'll get hundreds of comments and thousands and thousands of views, all just from flipping on Facebook Live. So to me, that's where it's at right now. Facebook Live is where the attention is.

Collaborate. If you are building a brand based on jokes, cooking, bikes, extreme sports, or bathing suits—*anything*—go to the top of Facebook and do searches on terms that are relevant to your business. Find the fan pages with the most followers, message them, and make them an incredible offer that makes it worth their while to share your original content on their platform or to work with you in other ways. For example, if you're a biker and you get a viral hit on your post about

---

* Especially if you're into sports. I predict that eventually there will be a sport that will be built from scratch through Facebook Live or maybe even some live platform that doesn't yet exist. It will upend the televised sports industry as we know it. Just watch.

how a motorcycle helmet saved your life, the best thing you could do would be to spend hours getting in touch with every single popular motorcycle fan page and offering them a brilliantly funny PSA about helmets to share on their page. Collaborating through Facebook is a strategic move that has enormous potential to quickly build your audience.

Imagine This

Let's say you're a newly divorced forty-two-year-old real estate agent named Sally living in Sacramento, California. There are so many people buying and selling properties out there. How are you going to stand out?

You start by creating a pillar piece of content. In this case, your ideal pillar would be a weekly audio podcast that people can listen to as they drive around town scoping out neighborhoods. Biweekly would be OK, and monthly would be better than nothing, but you know that the more content you put out, the more opportunities you can create. (Stay with me here—you'll see, Facebook is the star in this story.)

Your podcast explores the minutiae of daily living in and around Sacramento and establishes you as the "virtual-content mayor" of the city. Local residents tune in to hear your take on their beloved city. One day you might review restaurants and local dishes, on another you'll dig into the history of the city, and on another you'll interview local influencers. From then on, whenever anyone wants to know more about Sacramento or its future, everyone knows you're the person to contact, because you've made it clear that no one knows the city better or loves it more than you.

As you're doing your stories about the people, places, or things that make Sacramento a unique, vibrant place to live, you take notes and highlight details from each podcast that can be turned into ancillary pieces of content. For example, if you interview the superintendent of the school district and he mentions that five of its teachers recently received prestigious national awards, you've found another piece of content. Track down those five teachers, take their picture, and create a Facebook post that asks, "Did you know that five Sacramento School District teachers have been nationally recognized for excellence in education?" You include a link to your podcast interview with the school superintendent. More and more Sacramentans learn who you are and become regular listeners. When one of them finds out that his friend's family is moving to town because his wife got a job transfer, he forwards the podcast link so they can learn more about the school district. Suddenly, a family who will need to buy a home has your voice in their ear and your contact information at their fingertips. That cycle repeats over and over until, within five years, you're so established as the primo real estate expert of Sacramento that your new business comes in almost exclusively by referral.

Then you make more content. You go out and film or photograph the places you talk about in each podcast and post the files to Facebook. You link your podcast to the images, so that now people who don't already live in the city can see for themselves what these areas look like without having to go anywhere else on the Internet.

Now, who the hell is going to see this content when you're brandnew to the business and have only twelve followers, most of whom are family? Lots of people, because Facebook is the one place where you can spend unbelievably smart advertising dollars. Their targeting is unparalleled. You could spend maybe fifty bucks against all twentyfive-to-seventy-two-year-old Facebook users who live in Sacramento and potentially reach about ten thousand people. The details of the platform and its targeting capabilities are changing all the time, so you Google "How to run a Facebook ad" to get the most current rates and practices. Then, when people start commenting on your page or your content, you answer every single one, every single time (read *The*

Thank You Economy). When you've got no audience, you should be taking every opportunity to engage with people who are taking an interest in you. To do otherwise is absolutely bonkers. The fact that this needs to be said speaks to many people's audacity and laziness.

A podcast would be the best pillar for a real estate agent, but if you just can't get comfortable with that but you're an excellent writer, your pillar should be a weekly post for your blog, This Week in Sacramento, where you share all the same information I suggested for the podcast in written form, plus local real estate news updates. Now you're not just the virtual-content mayor of the city, but you're its newspaper, too.

You write a piece about the oldest doughnut shop in town. The owner mentioned that he was nervous about the new Walmart slated for construction right next door. You post that doughnut article. Then you draw (or pay someone twenty dollars to draw) a sketch of the corner where the doughnut shop is located, with a big Walmart logo drawn in. You post that arresting image on your Facebook feed as well; it's striking enough that anyone who cares about the shop or about Sacramento might stop to study it more carefully as it scrolls through their feed. People click the link attached to your blog post, which raises their awareness of who you are and what you do.

As a real estate agent, your pillar could also be a reality show like my DailyVee. You hire an intern or professional videographer to follow you around as you show homes, have meetings, negotiate deals, and interact with colleagues, as well as while you attend your son's baseball game or shop at the supermarket. You basically film a daily love letter (and occasional complaint, if necessary) to the city where you live and work, and share that love with your viewers, reality-star style.

Once you get comfortable with video, Sally, you try your hand at Facebook Live. Every Thursday from eight to nine p.m., Sacramentans and potential Sacramentans can find you in front of the camera ready to answer any questions they may have about the real estate market, neighborhoods, schools, doctors, tattoo parlors . . . all the people and places that make up a community. People enjoy being a part of your show, and you get to spread your knowledge, help people out, and build your brand. Everyone benefits.

You post each video to Facebook, then extract pieces to create hundreds of minivideos, like how to negotiate a contract, what to look for when touring a house, and home styling tips for the first-time seller.

While you're busy posting original content on Facebook, you're also joining as many Facebook communities as you can. You'll join the national ones for real estate agents, of course, but you also want to join the Sacramento mom groups—but not to sell, because you know that you should never ask for anything until you've given twice as much or more than you're hoping to get.* You join because you're a mom or because you want to be a mom or because you have nieces and nephews and want to stay on top of mom talk for them. If you're raising a family, you join other family-oriented groups. If you golf, you join the golfing groups. If you like Pokémon Go, you join the Pokémon Go Sacramento group. Get involved in all the lighthearted aspects of the city. If you engage like crazy and build your personal brand properly, people will learn that you're a real estate agent, but they won't shy away from you, because they'll know you as a human being first, just as they would if they'd met you in person. Once you become an influencer within these groups, members will check out your Facebook business page and contact you when they're ready to sell or buy a home.

This strategy sounds like a hell of a lot more work than just posing for a picture in front of a cute house while holding an Open House sign, doesn't it? It sounds a lot more interesting, too. Which strategy

---

* This is a crucial point, one that I outline in detail in another book, *Jab, Jab, Jab, Right Hook*. If you don't already understand the nuances of jabs and right hooks, pick up a copy and figure it out before you go acting like a slimeball.

do you think is going to attract the attention and loyalty of more consumers? You know the answer.

HOW I'M CRUSHING IT

Brittney Castro, Financially Wise Women

IG: @BRITTNEYCASTRO

Brittney Castro is creating a personal brand in one of those industries that pretty much discourages it at every turn: personal finance. She'd originally wanted to be an event planner, because she liked socializing and working with people. Math had always come easily to her, but she thought finance would be a dry, boring career. Yet when she was offered a job as a financial advisor, her career counselor suggested that the two fields might have more in common than she realized, because both involved helping people, and said that she'd never know for sure until she tried it. So she went to work at a large corporate firm, where for five years she clocked sixty to seventy hours per week. Her counselor was right—she did like the work. What she didn't like was the stress and the corporate environment. "A lot of that lifestyle just didn't match up with who I naturally was. I was sick all the time because I was trying to be somebody I'm not. I think it was that internal pressure of following the path that you're told to follow in life and realizing, this is not leading me to a happy life."

As the Great Recession hit, she started reading personal-development books; if she was going to work for a big chunk of her life, she figured she'd better find something that she enjoyed doing. At the same time, she noticed that women were starting YouTube channels devoted to beauty, makeup, and fashion, "And I thought, *Whoa, that looks so fun.*"

She realized that she did want to stay in finance—"I just needed more freedom to do it in a way that felt authentic to me." She set her sights on becoming the next Suze Orman.

> She's great, but she's for an older demographic. I'm a woman, I'm in finance—there's not too many of us— I'm young, and I'm half Hispanic, I better freaking play this up! It was a process though, because for so long, especially in finance and law, you're taught, "No, you can't, you can't, you can't." It was almost like breaking out of a shell and learning to find my own voice, learning how to be authentic online, but still professional. It's taken me years to find that comfort level.

The self-professed "business nerd" also fed on a steady diet of marketing and branding books. She read *Crush It!* right around the time that she moved to an independent firm where there would be more freedom to leverage an individual brand. In 2011 she launched a blog, a Facebook page, a YouTube channel, and a Twitter account. "I had to explain to them, it's the same thing as going to a workshop and teaching about money. The only difference is, it's a video on my YouTube channel. It was just turning what I was doing offline, online." But she still had to get every tweet and script preapproved. And yet, "even though it was a headache, it taught me how to be very thoughtful and intentional, and not just throw up stuff for the sake of it."

Two-and-a-half years later, Brittney left the firm to start

her own business, Financially Wise Women, catering to women and couples in their thirties and forties.

Not everyone was impressed, but she didn't care. In fact, the more her peers disapproved, the more she knew she was on the right path. For example, in 2015 she launched a finance rap video on YouTube.

A lot of financial advisors e-mailed me or commented to say, "This is so unprofessional," and, "You're using your CFP, your certified financial planner mark, in a way that's not appropriate." I do want to stay respectful, and I do use a compliance person, but when that feedback came, I was like, "Yes! That's exactly what I want to hear, because the video was not made for you. You're an old white guy in Wisconsin. This is for urban teenagers who like to watch *BuzzFeed* videos. I'm teaching them money principles in a fun and playful way. And they love it." I think there is some validity in listening to what others are saying, but I have to stay true to who I am and ultimately what my vision is for my business and my life.

Today she's on all the expected channels, but surprisingly, Facebook Live is a personal favorite. "I love live content. It's easy for me to set up a Facebook Live, connect with people, answer their questions. I think it brings them the most value and makes it the most real for them." She not only conducts Facebook Live sessions within her own Facebook groups and community, but has also done them with her brand partners, like Chase and Entrepreneur. She hopes one day to create an online live-stream video show that leverages all the communities she works with.

In the meantime, while some in her industry lob criticism at her, she's in demand as a consultant to other firms and advisors interested in learning more about how to market and brand themselves, even if only within a corporate structure. She also accepts a number of paid speaking opportunities each year. Other than that, she's got her head down.

I actually don't even care what others are doing in the industry. I never even really look. I just work on my company and my brand. Unless I go speak at a conference, I really don't connect with a lot of financial advisors. And I did that strategically, because when I first started the company, there was just so much outside noise. It's draining. It works a lot better because I'm not constantly comparing myself, or competing. I need to just do me.

Though I don't know Brittney, of all the contributors in this book, she's the one that means the most to me. People working in industries like pharma and law like to point the finger at strict regulations to explain why they're not crushing it on social media. But as you can see, where there's a will, there's a way. Brittney's success proves that when you take the time and effort to learn how to navigate toward your goals while still following the rules, you can go forward without fear.

13

INSTAGRAM

Except for YouTube, Instagram has created more famous people than any other platform. It's massive, it's a place where you can be equally successful as a content producer or a content curator, and it's the hottest social network in terms of scale and impact. Some would say it's gotten harder to get noticed there now that it's crowded; it's gotten so popular that college graduates are actually taking a year or two to see if they can get big on Instagram before trying to get a traditional job. It's not as flexible as Facebook, though I predict that very soon it will remove the time limits on videos. Although its content is bite-size like Twitter's, nothing in its structure makes it ideal for having conversations. Yet there are so many great tactics you can use to garner awareness—hashtags, collaborations, tagging, ads—that I believe the attention an influencer can enjoy here, especially skilled photographers, chefs, designers, and other artists, runs deeper than on Twitter or Facebook. I know it's true for the thirty-five-and-under crowd, and I suspect that the thirty-six-to-fifty-year-olds are starting to come around, because it's a newer, shinier, and maybe even happier place than their tried-and-true Facebook. Moreover, the importance of the platform doubled with the launch of Instagram Stories in August 2016.

Until then, Instagram was a highly curated place. That's one of the reasons people love it so much. Less polarized and politicized than Facebook, it's a place where you go to post the beautiful highlights of your days. That was a bit of a problem. In fact, on the day Stories launched, CEO Kevin Systrom admitted to *TechCrunch* that he hadn't posted anything to Instagram in the six days before the interview because "none of the moments seemed special enough." Meanwhile, the success of Snapchat Stories had proven that people were extremely interested in sharing the raw footage of their lives so long as they knew it wouldn't stick around to haunt them forever. So Instagram copied Stories and became a platform that gave users complete freedom to create as the mood moved them. They could put up a beautifully filtered photo and leave it up like a fine work of art or put up a piece of throwaway content that would be scrapped like the first draft of your last sales presentation.

It scaled fast. Snapchat had already laid all the groundwork in getting people comfortable with the idea of ephemeral content, so there was no learning curve to contend with, as is the usual case when platforms introduce new features. Instagram placed it at the top of the app, too, making it impossible for users to miss. In less than a year, Instagram Stories became one of the most popular features of one of the biggest platforms in the world, offering a dynamic place for users to create content to complement their perfectly curated Instagram feed.

There are many features that make Instagram a requirement for any budding influencer or entrepreneur. You can post for posterity, or you can post for instant gratification. You can draw and filter and caption and tag. Though the feature is currently available only to verified accounts, you'll soon be able to add links to your posts, a simple move that will open the floodgate of opportunities to drive people to your other content, whether it's on your website, your blog, or other social networks.

Anyone wishing to build a personal brand should be on Instagram. Create a profile now, or regret it for years to come.

7 Steps to Biz Dev

1. Make sure your Instagram is full of incredible content, the best you can make. More people are about to come see what you're about.

2. Search relevant keywords. For example, if you're building a biker brand, *motorcycles.*

3. Click on the first hashtag that shows up. As I write this, there are over 2.4 million posts with #motorcycles.

4. Click on every picture you see with that hashtag. The first four that show up in this instance belong to accounts that have a combined following of over one million Instagrammers.

5. Investigate every account and any linked websites to confirm that they are owned by people or companies in your field, or even if they're not, to check if they could use your services or products anyway.

6. Click on the three dots in the upper right corner of their pages and send those individuals or businesses a custom-written direct message. *Do not spam with cut-and-paste bullshit.* If that's the best you can do, you've already lost.

7. In your message, explain what drew you to them (I love your work; I've always admired you; you post the funniest memes; this post is so creative; etc.), why you are worth paying attention to (my goal is to promote better biker safety; I've designed a helmet even the most helmet-averse rider won't mind wearing; I've launched the freshest, most exciting biker-themed YouTube channel on the Internet), and what value you can offer (I'd like to send you one of my helmets to try; I'd love to invite you on air to talk about your new book, and I'd be honored if you'd let me make you a free video documenting your next ride; I can send you six bikers to model leather jackets on your vlog for free).

You can also target your search by location. Just type in the name of your city, sometimes even your neighborhood, and click Places or look for the location symbol in your list of top results. You'll see everyone who posted in your immediate area.

Do this—search, click, investigate, DM—for six to seven hours every day. Do it during every lunch break, every bathroom break, every time you're waiting for your child to get out of dance class, and in the twenty minutes you've got before the enchiladas come out of the oven. **Only a tiny fraction of the people you reach out to will respond.** That's all you need. With every successful contact, you increase your ability to prove yourself worthy of any attention at all, and you increase your visibility. Do this enough times, and the effect will snowball until suddenly you'll be the brand that people and businesses start reaching out to.

To see these instructions in action, go to the following post: GaryVee.com/GVBizDev.

Imagine This

Let's say your name is Rick, and you're a twenty-seven-year-old clothing store manager in Nashville, Tennessee. You're ambitious, and you're lucky enough to work for an organization that isn't interested in micromanaging your social-media accounts.* You start taking pictures of everything in the store—let's call it EnAvant—and everyone who walks in, if they will let you. You photograph the tops as they're being laid out on the shelves, the dresses as they're being hung, the shoes as they're being displayed. You photograph yourself in the

---

* I know that this is still a too common scenario. Many organizations simply cannot understand that it's in their best interest to let their employees be real on social media, and that the best way to control their online image is quite simply to be such an amazing brand and create such a supportive work environment that employees have only good things to say about them. Unless you work in law or finance, where the rules are a little different, here's my advice for those of you working for companies that won't allow you to express yourself online and create a personal brand, even on your own time: Leave as soon as you can, and go work for one that will. Better yet, start your own thing, as Brittney Castro did (see page 219).

men's fashions, adding your personal flair to every outfit, and you photograph your female employees in the women's clothing. You ask your customers if they'll pose for pictures in their new outfits. Then you post every picture on your Instagram account, accompanied by well-thought-out, relevant hashtags. You know that how you frame your images, or the techniques you use to give them a sense of fun or creativity and really show off the clothes, will be crucial to growing your fan base. But you can't build a fan base if you're not visible. Aside from getting influencers to mention you or your product, or paying for ads, you know that the fastest way for a brand starting at zero, like yours, is to master hashtags. If it's springtime, and you're posting a picture of a woman in a canary-yellow raincoat, you include the coat brand's hashtag, along with #EnAvantwear, #springfashion, #springlooks, #raincoat, #readyforrain, #yellow. As more people spot your work, in time you become known for your fashion sense and cheeky sense of humor.

You start reaching out to people who live in the vicinity of the store, but you don't use direct mail, because who's got money for that? And you don't hunt for the fashionistas and society people already appearing in the local culture-and-lifestyle glossies that document all the area fund-raisers and real estate development. Instead, every day during your lunch break, you open up your Instagram account and type in "Nashville, Tennessee." Up pop the most popular posts in the area. You click around on a few of the ones with the most followers to make sure they live in or around Nashville, and in particular, you look for pictures in these accounts that suggest the account owners would be interested in wearing pieces from your store. You then send them a direct message: "Hi, my name is Rick and I'm the manager of EnAvant. Love your look. Come by the store, we'd love to give you a gift certificate for 20 percent off."

In the time it takes you to finish your chicken salad, you've started building relationships with six new people who live near your store and have a proven interest in your product. You do this every day, five days a week. Of the thirty-two people you talk to every week, seven post a story about how this guy named Rick who works at EnAvant reached out to compliment their shoes, top, or hat, and offered them a discount at the store.

Maybe you go even further. You put together a fashion show and DM all the influencers in the area, as well as any locals whose Instagram account makes it clear they're really into clothes and accessories, and invite them to attend so they can see the new collection and get 30 percent off all in-store purchases. And then you make sure the event is so fun and special that people start posting pics of themselves and telling their followers where they're spending their evening.

Here's what happens next:

People start posting pictures of themselves on their own Instagram accounts and tagging you, the brand, and the store. Competitors start reaching out to find out if you're interested in re-creating some of your magic at their stores. Meanwhile, someone in EnAvant's upper management takes notice and realizes that she has an incredibly valuable employee in Tennessee whom she will do pretty much anything to keep.

Or:

By following up all this incredible word of mouth with impeccable customer service for those who venture into the store, in short order EnAvant becomes one of the hottest new stores in Nashville—and you catch the attention of fashion photographers and clothing designers all over the country.

Or:

Some of the brands you feature in your Instagram posts notice what you've done and reach out to find out if you're interested in helping them with their social media. That's another big win.

Or:

You have so much fun sharing your brand of visual storytelling that you decide you want to do it full-time, and you launch your own digital fashion magazine.

Not only can you build business for the store by biz-deving this way, but also you can make someone's day. Any or all of these scenarios could happen, and they could happen to you, whether you're a clothing store manager or work in retail of any kind, even in a restaurant. It all comes down to passion and proper execution.

HOW I'M CRUSHING IT

Brittany Xavier, Thrifts and Threads

IG: @THRIFTSANDTHREADS

It was supposed to be just a hobby, a creative outlet to practice with her new camera. That's what Brittany Xavier had in mind when she launched her blog, Thrifts and Threads, in December 2013. Even as a political science major, she'd always loved fashion and had made it a habit to follow trends and designers. Her look was a blend of high and low fashion, mixing ready-to-wear with vintage finds and select designer pieces. Upon graduation, she was accepted by several law schools, but, concerned that law school was incompatible with raising a toddler—her daughter, Jadyn, was only three years old—she instead went to work for an insurance marketer that would guarantee family-friendly hours. It paid the bills, and it wasn't too demanding. She often found herself finished with her goals for the day by four p.m. and had to find busywork to fill up the time until she could go home at six.

Even when they were dating, she and her husband, Anthony, also in marketing, had always had side hustles, such as buying items at discount stores and reselling them on Amazon. It was something they did as a couple, a shared activity that gave them a little sense of freedom. In addition, Anthony, who had developed an interest in Web design and social media in college, built websites. When he got a camera soon after they were married, they thought they'd go out and take pictures of themselves and their daughter, document their family life on a blog, and hopefully make a little money off the affiliate links. Xavier, always interested in style and fashion, would do the creative, and Anthony would take care of the back end of the blog.

The only reason Xavier started an Instagram account was to promote and bring traffic to the blog. She figured out that she was supposed to tag brands and use hashtags by looking at other accounts like hers. Six months in, when she'd accrued about ten thousand followers and was earning about $100 per month from the affiliate links on her blog, she started getting occasional calls from brands asking if they could send her some clothes so she could post photos of herself wearing some of their pieces. That's when she started doing some research and discovered that there was a whole strategy behind growing an Instagram account. She and Anthony stayed up late at night reading and listening to podcasts about online marketing. It was after reading *Crush It!* that they realized the blog could be more than just a fun hobby—an actual business.

That's when she started charging brands for posts. At first, one Instagram post with the brand mentioned in the caption was $100. If the brand simply wanted to be tagged, she'd charge $50. When the people on the other end of the phone expressed surprise, "Oh, only $100?" she knew she was underselling herself, so she upped her fee to $200 per post. Then one day, an established jewelry line e-mailed her and proposed one blog post and one Instagram post for a fee of $1,000.

Xavier wasn't a seasoned influencer yet, but she was smart enough to know that a company's first offer was almost always less than what it was ultimately willing to pay.

Again she raised her rates, and soon she was earning as much or more per day as she was at her insurance marketing job. After three months of matching her income, a year-and-a-half after starting the blog, she left her day job so she could network and accept more invitations for brand meetings and to preview new collections. There she also met other bloggers who were willing to answer questions and help her calculate her worth. At her husband's suggestion, she also started getting more personal on her blog, starting with a post titled "I Quit." The response was so overwhelming, in particular from other people wanting advice on how to start their own blogs, that she started posting weekly blogging tips. The first, "How I Started My Blog in 5 Steps," remains one of her most read posts.

Today Xavier has a manager who negotiates her fees and helps her get branding work, but she still tags brands she's wearing, and she only posts brands she really loves and believes in. The blog has also expanded from strictly fashion to a lifestyle brand. Xavier travels a lot for work, but she uses the opportunity to produce travel content on the go, photographing herself at hotels, resorts, and restaurants that she likes and that she thinks her readers will appreciate. For this reason, she has developed good relationships with a number of hotel brands, and now when she and her family travel on their own, their stays are usually comped. She is also frequently invited to visit openings of new resorts or hotels so she can share the experience with her readers.

In May 2016, Anthony quit his job, too, a move he announced in a blog titled "He Quit Too." The pair tries to shoot all their photos during the day so that they are available when their daughter comes home from school. Jadyn's life changed as well. Her father is present for every school event. She no longer attends after-school care. Sometimes brands request pictures of Brittany with Jadyn, especially for child-friendly or Mother's Day events or promotions. When that happens, Xavier's rate goes up, and she deposits a portion of the fee into an account created for Jadyn, which she's using to teach her ten-year-old the basic principles of financial literacy.

The multiple deadlines and the inability to turn off the machine, even for a short vacation, can create a lot of pressure. "I've been doing this for almost four years, the same thing every day. We're taking photos, we're shooting content, writing, thinking about future trends." But the couple's daughter helps keep everything in focus for them.

Having a child means that Xavier refuses more jobs than a lot of other lifestyle bloggers. It's not always an easy choice.

I turned down a really great job from a well-known jewelry line. They wanted me to attend a two-hour dinner, and post to Instagram and Facebook while I was there. The job was more than a three-month salary at my former full-time job. As far as posting requirements, this was one of the easiest jobs I probably could have booked, but I had agreed to go on a school trip to Sacramento with Jadyn. It was killing me, but I had to keep it in focus. The whole reason I did this was so I could go on these trips with Jadyn and be there for her. There will be other jobs.

The competition in the fashion and lifestyle blogosphere is fierce, but Xavier still sees room for newcomers. "Even though it is saturated, if you can do it in a unique way or have your own style, you can definitely stand out in the crowd. Brands are always looking for what's new. They're also pouring more money into [influencer marketing], because they're seeing more of the conversion of blogs versus a radio ad or a television ad, where they have no tracking. But through blogs, they're able to track exactly where the links are coming from and exactly the conversions.

"Brands are definitely catching on more, and the ones that are not using affiliates or not doing the campaigns are figuring out how they can get into that." In fact, digital ad sales are expected to surpass global TV ad sales by the end of 2017.

On screen Xavier and her family's life seems effortless, but she expresses surprise at how many people don't recognize how much work it takes to build a successful blog and Instagram account.

So many people write me and say, "I wrote a post and no one read it. So how would I grow that?" I'm like, "You didn't even do any consistent work." I worked so much on the weekends and nights while working my other job. I didn't go out with my friends. I didn't go out on dates. We literally stayed at home and worked on our computer after our daughter went to bed. It's a lot of writing; it's a lot of research. You don't just sign up. For the first year, I wasn't making any money, maybe $100 or $200 a month. It was nothing. People don't understand that part. They're like, "Why would you do it for a year when you see no return?" I was seeing a return on my readership, and my following was growing, and that was motivating me. But for someone starting a blog who wants to make it specifically for money, it's a hard way to start, because you're not passionate about what you're doing. You have to love what you do.

PODCASTS

Podcasts are a godsend for two reasons.

1. Most people aren't comfortable on camera. They think they look stupid. They worry about their hair, their glasses, or their makeup. They fuss over the lighting. None of it matters, but it's enough to distract them from concentrating on providing the best experience they can for their viewers. Podcasts are far less intimidating.

2. Podcasts sell time, which is why everyone, including people who rock on camera, should try to create one. In this hyperspeed world, multitasking is everything, and **it's a lot easier to listen to a podcast while you check your e-mails and pay your bills than to watch a video**. In addition, as of 2014, the 139 million total commuters in the United States spent 29.6 billion hours traveling to and from their workplaces. A lot of that commute time is spent in cars where drivers can't watch videos (for now). They can, however, easily listen to podcasts. In the information age, podcasts allow us to efficiently and effectively maximize our knowledge.

I've had a podcast since October 2014, right around the time that the podcast Serial, produced by NPR's *This American Life*, became a sensation and thrust podcasting into the mainstream. But the truth is, I wasn't following my own advice. At the time, I felt stretched too thin to produce yet another piece of original native content for a platform (yes, even I reach my limits sometimes), so all I did was put up the audio track from the AskGaryVee show. It didn't do badly—I was always in the Top 25 podcasts in the business category—but I knew with more attention it could do better. In December 2016, I finally figured out how to rebrand it as The GaryVee Audio Experience, which was liberating. Instead of exclusively posting AskGaryVee content, now I could post a rant I'd recorded into my phone while boarding a plane, a clip from one of my keynotes, or an excerpt that didn't make it into the DailyVee. Inserting variety and creativity helped the podcast's popularity surge. Today my podcast sits comfortably and consistently in the list of the Top 150 podcasts on Apple's Charts. Some of those who listen are brand-new to my content, and others already follow me on other channels. Either way, it gives me one more way to share my content, build my influence, and help people get started building the life they want.

Podcasts 101

Whether you're uploading onto Spotify, Apple Podcasts, SoundCloud, Stitcher, or any other podcast distribution platform, there will be very little you can do to differentiate one from another. You can run ads on Spotify and SoundCloud, but they're still extremely expensive. Other than that, as of this writing, there are really no original, creative ways to build a personal brand within the podcast platforms other than by producing the best content you can. You'll have to promote your show through your other social-media channels and encourage symbiotic relationships with others who have bigger platforms than you.

The good news, however, is that iTunes will open podcasting analytics, so podcasters will be able to see exactly where people pause, skip, or sign off within their content. This will be invaluable in helping you learn faster how you can better tailor your content to serve your audience what it wants.

Imagine This

Let's say you're a seventy-five-year-old woman named Blanche. Your best friend is Judy. You've been inseparable since you were young girls growing up on the same block, and you've never lived more than a few miles apart. The two of you have raised a combined total of six children, been married three times, buried one husband, taken twelve joint vacations, adopted eleven pets, and over the past ten years, the only time you've missed your monthly standing date for a movie and lunch at Ruby Tuesday was that time when Judy was hospitalized with gallstones.

One night, in line to buy candy before seeing *Wonder Woman* at the movie theater, Judy says she thought Kathleen Turner's best performance might have been when she did the speaking voice of Jessica Rabbit. Here we go again. One of the reasons you like going to the movies with Judy is that you two rarely agree on the merits of a film, and it makes for great debate over burgers and fries afterward. But this time she's taken you by surprise. You raise your eyebrows so high they climb right over your hairline. Better than Turner's role in *Romancing the Stone*? Better than *Prizzi's Honor*? Better than *Peggy Sue Got Married*? Judy holds firm. As you bicker, you can hear people chuckling behind you. Someone says, "They're the new Siskel and Ebert."

That gives you an idea. After the movie, you and Judy head over to your favorite quiet corner at the local RT, but before the two of you exchange your thoughts about *Wonder Woman*, you pull out your iPhone and hit the voice memo button. You record your conversation. You go home, and the next day you call your nephew, who has a podcast about muscle cars, and ask him how to upload your "tape" onto the Internet. He gently informs you that you're going to need to upload the MP3 file onto a podcasting platform, and that if you can wait until the weekend he'd be happy to show you a few simple steps and teach you to use the basic equipment you'll need to get set up. If you can't wait, he says, you can find all the information you need on the Internet. "Just Google how to upload a podcast and distribute it." You decide to wait, but in the meantime, you call Judy and tell her that you want to go to the movies again next week.

Thus begins the Blanche and Judy Show, a movie review podcast in which two elderly ladies share their thoughts on movies past and present. Your personalities, deep friendship, and chemistry make it a riot for listeners, but you also make it uniquely 2018 by recording your conversations in the theater before the movie starts, on such topics as your strong conviction that Raisinettes are a disgrace to the grape and Judy's memories about the ushers that used to escort ladies to their seats. You also interview four people as they walk out of the film to get their take.

In three short years, yours is one of the Top 150 podcasts on Apple. The podcast is your pillar, but you use it to create microcontent, too. Judy's sense of humor is often good for a quote, so you create memes and post them on Facebook and Instagram. You engage with people on Twitter and raise awareness of the podcast there. The two of you are interviewed by *Entertainment Weekly* and *Variety*. In time, it gets harder for you to get out of the house every week—your back often aches, and you're most comfortable in your La-Z-Boy—but it doesn't matter anymore because the studios are sending you and Judy their movies to preview. Thanks to the branding opportunities that have come your way, all of your living expenses are more than easily covered, and you are thrilled to know that you will be able to pass much more of the savings you and your husband accrued over a lifetime to your family.

HOW I'M CRUSHING IT

John Lee Dumas, Entrepreneurs on Fire

IG: @JOHNLEEDUMAS

"I was dying a slow death in the cubicle."

Sound familiar?

If you're still young or in school, is it something you are trying like hell to avoid?

"I had this whole world of creativity inside of me, but I wasn't able to use any of it. I felt like I was almost choking on my own creativity because I had to be in a suit and tie and very formal. Everything was black and white, and I needed some color in my life."

Until he turned thirty-two, John Lee Dumas's life had been as traditional as apple pie. The grandson of two military veterans and the son of a JAG officer, service to his country was in his blood. He left his small town in Maine in 1998 on an Army ROTC scholarship to major in American Studies at Providence College in Rhode Island. A member of the first round of officers commissioned after 9/11, a year to the day after graduating college, he started a thirteen-month tour of duty in Iraq. He spent four years on active duty before returning to the civilian world. He was at the start of a four-year stint as a captain in the reserves, but otherwise he had no idea what to do with himself.

He tried law school but dropped out six months later. He then worked in corporate finance for a few years, but when he'd look at the people working in the positions above him, he knew he didn't want their jobs. He had a feeling that he was destined for entrepreneurship, but he didn't know what it really entailed or how to even begin. So he started reading self-help and business books. In 2009, one month after its publication, he read *Crush It!* That was the book that inspired him to quit the finance job, move to San Diego (where he'd never been), and become a real estate agent.

He kept at it for three years, but the job still didn't feel like a perfect fit. He kept rereading *Crush It!* every year, though, and in 2012, something new struck him. I emphasized that, no matter what industry you worked in, you had to build a personal brand. He realized that he wasn't doing that at all. He had a personal Facebook page, but he wasn't even on LinkedIn or Twitter in any professional capacity. So he knew that needed to change right away.

The other thing that caught his attention was the idea of podcasting. He wasn't really sure what a podcast was, so he decided to research it. He discovered that they were free and offered focused, targeted content. All those self-help books and audiobooks were getting expensive, and now he had to listen to even more if he was going to build a personal brand. Podcasts sounded like they were right up his alley.

"And that's when I fell in love with the medium. I became a super-consumer. For eight months, I listened to as many podcasts as I could. And it struck me that, jeez, I'm driving to work every single day, I'm hitting the gym multiple times per week—I need to find that seven-day-a-week show that interviews an entrepreneur and talks about their failures, lessons learned, aha moments. So I went to iTunes to find that show. It didn't exist! And I thought, *I can't believe this*. Why not be the person to create that show?"

So what if he had no experience in production or interviewing people? "I thought, *Well, if I do a daily show, I'll get better quicker*. Because all these people, they're doing four episodes a month with their weekly shows. I'm going to be doing thirty episodes a month. I just need to step into this void and do it, and I'm going to be bad. I'm going to do a hack job for a decent amount of time. And you can listen to today's podcast and go back to episode 15, and you can see, this guy isn't the same person. I was so bad. I was nervous, I was naïve. I was just hacking my way through it. But I kept doing it every single day."

He didn't just turn on a mic and start talking. Instead, he researched, diving into YouTube, absorbing all the free content and advice made available by other podcasters, and he found two mentors. Unnervingly, both strongly advised against doing a daily show, explaining that they made all their money doing other things beside podcasting. A daily show would preclude all those other activities. It was the only piece of advice Dumas rejected.

"I was like, 'You don't understand. I'm so bad that if I did do what everybody else is doing, nobody's going to listen. It's just not going to be good. So I have to do something different. I have to be unique. I have to do something that's going to raise people's eyebrows.' "

Those two mentors, with their large virtual Rolodexes, were invaluable to helping Dumas land his first interviews. They weren't going to introduce him to A players, but they were willing to introduce him to the B, C, and D players who were still building an audience, publishing books, and eager to share their stories with a neophyte in exchange for additional exposure.

It might sound as though Dumas has more confidence than the average human. Yet despite his conviction that podcasting every day—learning by doing—would be the best way to create a quality product, and despite many of his early guests' relatively low profiles and the public's almost immediate positive response, Dumas found himself almost paralyzed by imposter syndrome. Who was he to reach out to anyone for a one-on-one conversation? But he soldiered on and worked through his doubts and fears.

I started my entrepreneurial journey with one strength, and that was discipline, and I can tie that directly back to the army. But discipline alone is not going to get you anywhere. The two biggest areas I had to develop to go along with discipline were productivity and focus. People who are "just disciplined" can do something all day long, but what if they're producing the wrong content? That's where productivity has to come in. And you're not going to be able to consistently produce the right content unless you're able to block out what I call the weapons of mass distraction.

He launched his podcast, Entrepreneurs on Fire, in September 2012. As his guests shared their interviews with their sizable audiences, the podcast started ranking on the iTunes New and Noteworthy list. The dual effect meant that within two-and-a-half months the podcast drew over a hundred thousand unique downloads. He started receiving invitations to conferences, which gave him greater credibility and, along with his rapidly growing numbers, the opening to approach bigger names, such as Seth Godin and Tim Ferriss, who had both just released new books, Barbara Corcoran, and yes, Gary Vaynerchuk.

Now he was ready to explore ways to monetize. He turned to his audience and asked them what they wanted, and he listened.

> What I found very clearly was, if you are willing to commit to delivering free, valuable, and consistent content, you are going to build an audience from that. Then, if you are willing to engage that audience one-on-one and ask them, "What are you struggling with?" and then just listen, they will tell you what their pain points are, their obstacles, their challenges, their struggles. And then you, the person that they know, like, and trust, who's been delivering that free, valuable, and consistent content for a significant amount of time, can provide the solution in the form of a product, or a service, or a community.

And he did. Like Pat Flynn, each month he publishes a breakdown of what the business earns from his various revenue streams, which all add up to anywhere from around $200K to $300K per month. He also analyzes the company's successes, so other people can emulate them, and all the mistakes they've made, including money lost, so people can avoid making them.

Despite being a millionaire several times over, Dumas still reads *Crush It!* every year.

> The thing that keeps coming back to me is the land-grab. That's what I think so many people miss. All the time, people say, "John, you're so lucky that you

started podcasting when it was nothing and now it's the golden age of podcasting. You had the landgrab." And they're completely right. My timing was perfect. It was super amounts of luck and great timing, but what they miss is that there's always that next thing. They're not focusing on the next thing; they're looking at the past and there's the next Snapchat, then there's Instagram Stories, now there's Facebook Live. There's always that next opportunity to landgrab and to become that person. Yes, I'm considered the "king of podcasting" in a lot of niches because I've been able to build a seven-figure business around just podcasting. But since I've launched my podcast, there have been people that have become the king of Periscope, and then the king of Snapchat, and the king of Instagram. Things that didn't even exist when I launched my podcast. And while people were saying, "John, I just missed the boat with podcasting," I'm like, "Yeah, but you've also missed the boat with all these other things." So what I learned from Crush It! and continues to be relevant to me is, always keep your eyes on that horizon.

VOICE-FIRST

This may be my favorite chapter. Chances are good that most people reading have at least heard of, if not experimented with, all the platforms we have discussed so far in this book. But few of you at the time of this writing are probably sitting around thinking, *What's my Alexa Skill gonna be?* And yet you should, because we're about to talk about a tech innovation that I am absolutely sure will transform how the world consumes content. It's called Voice-First, and anyone currently building a personal brand needs to learn about it fast and early. Its platforms are the equivalent of yet-to-be-discovered Malibu beachfront property, much like Twitter in 2006, Instagram in 2010, and Snapchat in 2012.

I day-trade attention, and lately I am particularly interested by what people pay attention to during the transitions of their day, especially the three that occur in the home: what they do during the first fifteen minutes of their morning, the first fifteen minutes after they come home from work, and the last fifteen minutes before they go to sleep at night. Those are transition periods. They're the moments when we take stock, get updated, and plan for the next few hours of our lives. We're busy, so we want to do it fast. There was a time you'd pull out a pen and paper and start a to-do list, turn on the radio, or even check an app. Now, though, you don't even have to do that. All you have to do is talk.

Podcasts fill our brains during the long periods when we're quiet, such as while we drive or travel. Voice-first platforms are going to allow us to fill our brains during all the interstices of our lives, those blips of time that used to be lost to forgettable activities like brushing our teeth, sorting through mail, or even checking our phone notifications. In 2016, Google revealed that 20 percent of searches on its mobile app and Android devices are done by voice. That number is only going to rise, fast. And you have an amazing opportunity to make sure your brand rises with this trend.

As of this moment, there are two key players: Amazon Alexa, played through a device called the Echo, and Google Assistant, played through its Google Home device. Microsoft, Apple, Samsung, and others are preparing to make their respective pushes into the space with platforms of their own, but at this time it makes sense to focus only on the big two. I started with Alexa, launching a Flash Briefing Skill called GaryVee365. A Flash Briefing is a short report offering users a key bit of information. Mine offers daily motivation from yours truly. The Skimm's airs its breakdown of the day's top news stories; eHow's presents daily life hacks. Add these and others to your list of Flash Briefings, and when you ask for them, either by saying, "Alexa, give me my Flash Briefings," or even, "Alexa, what's in the news?" you'll hear from your favorite sources one after another.

Other Skills offer more interactive experiences. Enable *The Tonight Show* Skill (as opposed to the Flash Briefing) and you could ask for Jimmy Fallon's most recent monologue, but you could also get the most recent *Tonight Show* guest list or a rundown of his newest Thank-You Notes, a popular segment on the show where he expresses gratitude for anything from Pop-Tarts to Ryan Gosling. I could develop a Skill called GaryVee Recommends Wine that recommends three wines to go with whatever you told it you were going to eat and gives you the ability to order those wines straight from the Skill through a third-party alcohol delivery service like Drizly or Minibar Delivery or from my family wine shop, Wine Library.

What we're seeing with the development of Voice-First is the culmination of our addiction to speed. The world moves fast and we want to keep up. If there is a choice between reading a notification or checking an app and getting the same information via Voice-First, which allows us to keep our hands free and multitask, the latter is what we're going to pick. Just like the first washing machines and coffeemakers, Voice-First platforms will save people time. Once the masses understand that, they are going to flock to them. Be there ready and waiting when they do.

Your Flash Briefing will be a one-minute version of your one-hour podcast, a one-minute audio version of your eight-minute videos or live streams, or a one-minute selection of your pretty pictures on Instagram. You can bring people so much value right now, whether you create for Google, Amazon, or both. While brands have developed countless Skills, most deliver the same basic experience. The field is clear for anyone who is clever enough to come up with something fresh and new. Take the landgrab, my friends, and become a vital part of your consumers' morning routines. Very soon, as even more brands jump onto these platforms, it will get harder to make a dent in people's awareness. Don't let this moment pass. Don't let the big guys snap up all the cheap real estate. Please, put down this book right now and go create your Skill. Your one-minute audio tip of the day could be the thing that compels a person to put on your podcast during their morning commute instead of their usual NPR or classic rock.

Skills 101

▶ Keep your content super brief.

▶ Make it native. Do not do what I did with my original podcast when I just transferred the audio from a video onto the podcast platform. Tailor your content to suit the reason people are coming, which is to get fast, easily digestible information nuggets. "Hey, Alexa users . . ."

▶ Make it the highest quality possible. I cannot stress how important it is that you not treat your Skill as a dumping ground. It's great to collect the scraps from your other content so they don't go to waste, but study each piece closely and use your imagination and creativity to craft something new and fresh with them.

You know how it's such an irritating process to get off an e-mail list? First, you have to bother to go to the bottom of the e-mail and hunt for the unsubscribe button. Then you have to plod through a box asking if you are absolutely sure you want to leave, and would you care to share the reason? And then finally, upon confirming that you've been unsubscribed, you're told it could take a few business days before the e-mails stop coming.

In Voice-First, all people will have to do once they lose interest in your content is say, "Alexa, remove MumboJumbo's Flash Briefing," and boom, it will be done. You will have no room for error. No room to be annoying or too long or low quality. Go ahead and document the process while you learn how to craft your content—you can use clips from all that material for other content—but make sure whatever segment you publish is short and tight. You will need to be remarkable right out of the gate, or in three milliseconds, you'll be shut down.

Voice-First is going to become a huge pillar in our communications. By the time this book is published, Amazon Alexa, Google Assistant, Apple Siri, or some other platform will be talking to us in our cars. Remember when we all thought it was amazing that we could be driving along, recall that we used to love Kenny Rogers's "Lady," and download his greatest hits as soon as we got to our destination (because we would never do that while driving, right?). Soon, we won't have to wait to play a song or pull over to type in a location on a map app. We'll just tell Alexa what we want her to do, and she'll do it. Finally, texting and driving will be a thing of the past—unless we're in our driverless cars.

Skills 201

There is no Skills 201. The feature is so new, we're only just now identifying best practices. I hope you'll share yours with me as you discover them and explore all the exciting possibilities in this space. Hit me up at @garyvee.

My intuition is that all the brands in the how-to space will flock to Voice-First by 2020, and they will battle to be the ones chosen to teach people to make cookies and pair wine and get better at chess and clean carpets. It'll be our on-the-go resource, too. When changing our oil in the garage, we won't pull out the car manual or Google "How to change your oil." We'll just call out, "Tell me how to change my oil," and the Voice-First technology sitting on a shelf or mounted on the wall will ask us what kind of car we drive, then walk us through the process with step-by-step instructions. Right now we're putting Voice-First tech in only one or two rooms in the house. In the future, we won't go anywhere without it.

Imagine This: Alexa Skills

Let's say you're a forty-nine-year-old etiquette coach named Marlo. You used to think you'd be educating children in the finer points of polite conversation and the continental style of eating, but over time your services have been increasingly sought out by companies desperate to fill in the educational gaps of their millennial hires. They just don't know anything about proper protocol, especially for international business or formal affairs. Your business is doing OK, but things are starting to feel routine.

You're at your boyfriend's house one morning, and you hear him ask Alexa to tell him what's in the news. A seemingly human voice reads the morning headlines, then the weather, some sports stats, and a fun fact of the day, all from different media outlets.

Fun fact of the day? That's not news; that's just learning for the sake of learning.

A lightbulb goes on.

You spend the next few weeks recording the answers to every etiquette question you can think of. How do you fold a napkin for a formal table? Should I invite my boss to my birthday dinner? What's the best icebreaker question? How do I end a conversation at a cocktail party without being rude? Can I wear black sneakers with a black suit? You could have asked your phone these questions, but you look up "How to build an Alexa Skill" online and learn that there's a studio just a few miles away that will help you record the audio file. You upload your new Alexa Skill, The Manners Maven, and announce it to your clients and on all your content channels. They love the way the platforms let them engage with you in a virtual one-on-one. It gives them confidence. Eventually, you add "calls to action" to direct people to other pieces of your content on the Internet so they can discover longer versions of the answers they got from you here, as well as guest posts from other experts and interviews with people sharing their funniest, most awkward faux pas.

Imagine This: Flash Briefings

Let's say you're a thirty-seven-year-old landscaper named Johnny. Your business, Johnny's Landscape Art, nets around $200,000 per year. You decide that you need to boost your brand awareness, so you launch eleven Flash Briefings: Johnny's Daily Yard Tips—Zone 1, Johnny's Daily Yard Tips—Zone 2, and so on. Every day of the year, you offer the country seasonal information that will help gardeners tend their yards better, tailored for each of the eleven USDA plant hardiness zones, which are based on a region's minimum temperatures. "It's April 21, and spring has sprung. Zone 4, you're going to want to start fertilizing those spring bulbs. Zone 9 friends, I want you to consider planting citrus. Zone 6, now that your forsythia is blooming, make sure not to wait too long to prune it, or it'll be scraggly next year." You're the first of your kind on Amazon, and you're really good at this. The love you have for your work and your playful nature come through bright and shiny to the gardeners and homeowners who add one of your Flash Briefings to their morning lineup.

Meanwhile, Yvette in Seattle is in charge of curating the Alexa Skills Store, and she is bored. Every Flash Briefing is the same news-tech-weather-sports shit over and over and . . . wait a minute. What's this Johnny's Daily Yard Tip? Well, that's different. Different is good. She features one of them on the Skills page.

And this, *this*, is why you want to create content for Alexa now. What Facebook did for social-network games and Apple did for apps, Amazon is going to do for Skills and Flash Briefings. They're going to run commercials to raise awareness about their new product. Can you imagine if your voice is the one the whole country hears as an example of a great Flash Briefing? It could do for you what Apple's choosing to play "1234" in their 2007 iPod Nano commercial did for Feist.

Here's the very best part. You know how I'm always telling you that everything I want you to do is going to be hard and take scads of patience? Not this time. It will not take you too much time or effort to be discovered for creating a Flash Briefing because of the early novelty. It will five years from now, however. Five years from now, everyone will have a Flash Briefing, and it's highly unlikely that yours will get noticed without marketing the living shit out of it to get exposure. Five years from now, the moment will be gone. Do. Not. Wait.

Because you know what else happens to you, Johnny? Your Flash Briefings are featured, take off, and suddenly you get an e-mail from Cindy in Missouri, asking if you're interested in franchising your now nationally known brand. Within two years, your $200,000-a-year landscaping business is collecting a $25,000 check each year from seven hundred people all over the country.

Incidentally, Marlo the Manners Maven should do this, too, in addition to making her Skill. She should make a new recording of 365 etiquette questions, one for every day of the year. Did you know that even in the digital age, a handwritten thank-you note should always be sent after a job interview? Did you know that the word *etiquette* is derived from the French word for "ticket" and King Louis XIV's attempts to keep visitors from trampling his gardens? She needs to do this for the simple reason that she can, because the cost of Internet real estate today is still so, so low. Don't be the 2017 first-time home buyer in Malibu; be goddamn Thomas Jefferson buying about eight hundred thousand square miles of Louisiana Territory for three cents an acre in 1803 dollars (skipping the part about screwing the Native Americans already living on that land).

On the Horizon

While I was working on this book, Amazon announced that it had bought Whole Foods for just over $13.4 billion. We all woke up to the news and thought, *How the fuck did* that *happen?* It never should have. Whole Foods should have bought Amazon. There was a time twenty years ago when Whole Foods was a much bigger business than Amazon, and when your company is that much bigger than someone else's, with that much of a lead, yours should never lose. If it does, it's because your opposite number innovated ahead of you.

To those who think they don't have to invest in all the platforms because they're concentrating their efforts where they're seeing the most ROI, I say you're being foolish. I can think of several bloggers who were massively popular in 2004. It was the new frontier, and they had positioned themselves front and center, but they ignored the rise of YouTube and podcasts and Twitter, and now they're irrelevant.

They found something that worked and preferred to rest on their laurels rather than stay hungry and sharp. **They thumbed their noses at traditional media, but then they became traditional media.**

We see it all the time. ESPN made *Sports Illustrated* look old. *Bleacher Report* is in the process of making ESPN look fusty. *Barstool Sports* is already starting to make *Bleacher Report* feel stale. It happened to Macy's. It happened to Radio Shack, Woolworth's, Tower Records, Nokia . . . They crushed, they stagnated, they died. They are no different from any brand crushing it today. One day we could have a WTF moment upon hearing that Ralph Lauren filed for Chapter 11 bankruptcy protection or that *GQ* no longer exists. Learn the lesson now: everyone is playing the same game. If you don't play offense all the time, every day, every year, no matter how successful you become, someday you will wind up playing defense.

You have to keep looking ahead. I've got my eye on Marco Polo, Anchor, After School, AR (augmented reality), VR (virtual reality), and AI (artificial intelligence). You know what's going to happen? One day there's going to be a little ball hanging above every single human being's head recording everything they do. Swear to God, it's going to happen. Maybe it'll be a camera embedded in your body. I don't know the details, but I know that recording and documenting every minute of our lives will seem perfectly normal one day. You might think it sounds awful, and even scary, but just imagine if you could watch your grandmother right now. Imagine seeing her move through her life as a young woman, watching her fall in love with your grandpa, raising her kids, your mom, or starting a new job—not as though you're watching a movie, but feeling as if you're physically moving through her world with her. That's how real the technology is going to be. The question is not if but when.

The passion I have deployed around Alexa Flash Skills is the same passion I had for Twitter and YouTube in 2008 when I wrote this book's mother, *Crush It!*, back when the masses didn't know what the fuck I was talking about. Now people know what I'm talking about when it comes to Twitter and Instagram and YouTube, but they aren't doing the next step. They aren't tasting and trying and experimenting. They're leaving that up to me. They shouldn't. They should be out there with me trying things out for themselves.

You shouldn't have to turn to me to ask what's next. What do *you* see? All I'm doing is looking toward the horizon to see what platforms are capturing people's attention and altering their behavior. If I see something that is performing consistently, I take a closer look, and then a longer look, and then I start to execute. That's all you have to do, too. I don't have second sight; I just have a lot more patience than you do.

HOW I'M CRUSHING IT

Andy Frisella, The MFCEO Project

IG: @ANDYFRISELLA

Andy Frisella looks like a man who could squash your head like a grapefruit. For someone in his line of work, that's a good thing. Built and buff, his face lightly scarred from a long-ago knife attack, Andy is the founder and CEO—actually, the MFCEO (I'll let you guess what the MF stands for)—of two companies dedicated to fitness and health. A voracious reader, he found *Crush It!* by chance. He regularly buys books as they come out on Amazon regardless of whether he's heard good things about them or not, figuring that if he can glean even one or two useful pointers or thought-provoking ideas from each, his time has been well spent. At the time of *Crush It!*'s publication, Andy had already been in business ten years, selling sports nutrition products through his Missouri-based brick-and-mortar chain, Supplement Superstores (S2). Despite eight locations, S2 was doing what most businesses do—treading water. Business was good but not great, certainly not enough for Andy to take home more than about $50,000 a year. It was all a single guy at the time needed to pay the rent and enjoy dinner out every now and then, but Andy's ambitions had been significantly bigger when he and his business partner, Chris Klein, had launched the original store. All his life, Andy had been entrepreneurial, selling baseball cards, snow cones, even lightbulbs door-to-door. He liked making money, and he was frustrated that he couldn't get the business to grow faster. Yet although he wasn't bringing in the returns he'd thought he would, it was sure better than working for somebody else. No matter what, he wasn't about to give up and go get a "real job." So Andy decided that if doing something else wasn't an option, he'd need to focus on the part of the business that he did enjoy—helping people create their stories. Customers would visit his stores and return six months later completely transformed after using the knowledge and products they'd taken home with them. Some had lost as much as a hundred pounds; many had dramatically changed their lives.

So Andy doubled down on doing right by his customers, making sure they left his store feeling confident and equipped with everything they needed to achieve their goals. Store traffic immediately picked up.

Everybody knows when they're being sold. No matter how slick and cool and shiny a salesman is, customers recognize a fucking salesman. We all know them. And so when you have somebody who genuinely cares, people feel the difference. They feel it in the conversation and in their heart. And it has to come from a genuine place, or it doesn't work.

It was around this time that he found *Crush It!*, which also talked about caring about customers and focusing on what you are providing others as opposed to focusing on yourself. It was a pivot point, reinforcing his instincts and confirming that he was taking the business in the right direction.

I was passionate about making money, and that's what held me back for so long. I wanted to make money so bad that all I cared about was making money, like most of these dudes who are trying to start businesses. And when you're always focused on the money, you don't really think about what you could do better for your customers. When I shifted that focus and started caring about the customer in front of me, things started happening. I'm not super passionate about bodybuilding, I'm not a workout freak. I work out and stay in good shape, but it's just part of what I do so I can do other things. I'm passionate about creating people's success stories.

Andy and Chris reallocated a large chunk of their marketing budget to improving their in-store customer transactions. They handed out free T-shirts. They hired extra staff to advise people on their nutrition. They kept a clutch of umbrellas by the door for people to take with them if it started to rain. In short, they provided a customer experience completely different from what most people are used to.

Their business doubled. Every year. For five years in a row.

Eventually they increased their advertising and marketing budget. "Advertising should be used to accelerate the stories that are being told about you. People were finding us, coming into our company, staying, and referring their friends. If people aren't telling good stories, all advertising is going to do is speed your death."

The year 2009 also saw Andy and Chris start another company, 1st Phorm, a premium brand of supplements. This one was founded from the get-go on the principles Andy had finally realized were critical to business success.

The marketing strategy to build 1st Phorm was simple and grassroots—care about the customers, give them exactly what they want and more, and then create opportunities for them to easily tell others about their great experience. That's where social media came in. Andy had been on Facebook for a while but hadn't been using it properly. Now he took a strategic approach, going heavy on valuable content instead of constant pictures of his dog (though Andy's dogs still get plenty of screen time, and deservedly so), creating a place where his community could come together. In addition, he started building his personal brand. He tried Twitter but struggled to cram everything he wanted to say into 140 characters, so though @1stPhorm has a healthy following, you won't find Andy himself there. He calls Snapchat an "edifying" tool because it allows the world to see the real-life, behind-the-scenes work of entrepreneurship, though he admits he uses Instagram Stories more now. As for Instagram, he did exactly the opposite of what normally works best on the platform (to great effect—he has over six hundred thousand followers).

I post pictures and videos and make long-ass captions. And when I first started it, people told me, 'Oh, nobody wants to read this shit,' but apparently they do. With social media, I think it's more about being authentic to yourself and finding what's going to be the thing that suits you best, versus where everybody is and deciding that's where you need to be. It's about finding what works and working with that.

Together, the companies grew from $1 million in sales to $100 million. Andy predicts that 2018 will see in excess of $200 million.

As his brand and businesses swelled, people started to notice that Andy knew something other entrepreneurs didn't. The press reached out to get his story, and the more he shared, the more people wanted to know. He met a writer, Vaughn Kohler, who suggested he write a book. He was ready, so the two sat down for a series of interviews. They videotaped their sessions, and Andy thought some clips might make good content for Instagram and Facebook. Jackpot. "They started going crazy. I had one that got two or three million views, and it was a fifteen-second clip!"

After each post, Andy would get messages from people asking where they could hear the full podcast, so Andy figured he'd better start producing one. In June 2015, he and Kohler started cohosting The MFCEO Project, a motivational podcast about business and success. The first episode debuted at number one, and the program has stayed in the Top 50 in the managing and marketing category on iTunes since that day, earning 1.5 million downloads per month. Andy's persona and fiery delivery made him a natural for the speaking circuit, and the invitations started flooding in. He enjoys public speaking so much that he accepts every opportunity he can, "whether it's five people or five thousand." Sometimes when he's moved to do so, he speaks for free; sometimes he gets a $50,000 fee for a single event.

Starting in spring 2017, he launched a YouTube channel, The Frisella Factor, on which he answers his podcast listeners' e-mailed questions.

It took eighteen years for Andy to get to where he is now, and he envies the younger generation of entrepreneurs, who have never known a world where they couldn't connect to the bigger world with the click of a mouse. However, he also thinks that the younger generation would do well to remember that certain values and business practices are timeless.

My journey took much longer than it should have. We created our first business pre-social media, building everything through real word of mouth. Our second business was created post-social media. So we've done it in both eras. And the reason that we're successful is because the lessons we learned pre-social are applicable to post-social; you just have to use the tools the right way to accelerate the word of mouth. But if you're starting out right now, if it takes you seventeen years, there's something wrong with your brain. You can reach people instantly, and you get instant feedback. All the things that took us months and years to figure out could be known in a short amount of time. Now you can connect with people all over the world on a minute-by-minute basis. The kids now that are starting out are lucky.

But they're handicapped, too. They rely too much on the social. They rely too much on the likes, the shares, the messaging, and not enough on the face-to-face interactions. And learning how to create customer experience comes from face-to-face, man. You know, seeing somebody's eyes light up, seeing somebody smile, seeing somebody reach out and shake your hand and say, "Thank you so much for helping me with this. I really appreciate it." That's shit you can't get through the Internet. Unless they can go through that process, they're always going to be trying to automate. And that's why you see so many people creating a product that they sell, versus creating a true brand that represents something. If you can bridge these two things together [the social media smarts with the skills to engage face-to-face with empathy and care], you've really got something special.

CONCLUSION

I'm often asked what I've learned in the years since I published *Crush It!* The answer is this: I was right. Social media does equal business. Innovation makes people uncomfortable. We should care desperately about everything, yet not care at all what anyone else thinks. Someone will always be trying to tear you down. Talent has little value without patience and persistence. Success takes a shitload of work, and the people who ultimately break through and crush it are those who get all that and go for their dreams anyway.

I want you to find your courage and go for it. Somewhere out there is a middle-aged engineer, a single-parent exterminator, or a department store sales clerk trying to get through school who is reading this book and thinking, *Man, I fucking hate this job. But I love pizza. I'm going to start a YouTube channel and become the next Mario Batali.* People will think it's a ridiculous idea, just as people thought I was ridiculous when I wrote *Crush It!* But it's not ridiculous. It's not even sweetly optimistic. The proof is in the pudding. When I wrote *Crush It!*, I was basically just telling the world what I had done to grow a wine store in New Jersey. Now as I write, I'm a judge on Apple's first original show.

I hope this book has inspired you to change your life for the better. People often tell me they want to be like me. I'd rather you be like you, but if you really want to be like me, quit being a student of entrepreneurship and start doing the goddamn work. If you do, this will be the last business book you'll need to read. Success will happen faster for some people than for others, but if you're loving life and doing what you feel you were born to do, you'll be going in the right direction. Stay the course. It pays to be brave. If it helps, think of me as the shield between you and all the negativity out there. Believe me, I've heard every criticism and weathered every insult. I've had to defend my position thousands of times, and I've faced disappointments. I've taken all the punches, and I'm not only still standing, but I'm stronger than ever. There is nothing anyone can throw at you that they haven't already thrown at me. If I can stomach it, so can you—if you want to crush it badly enough.

Remember, you're not trading in your day job for an easier life—there's nothing easy about becoming an entrepreneur and influencer. You're trading it in for a different life, one with more flexibility and fun. Chad Collins (Twitter: @chadcollins) credits *Crush It!* with helping him create his seven-figure companies and two Guinness World Record–breaking fan festivals, LEGO Brick Fest Live and Minefaire, out of a YouTube channel he created with his seven-year-old daughter. Collins actively tried to avoid the entrepreneurial life, because he knew how hard it could be. "I grew up in a family of entrepreneurs, and when it was going well, awesome. When it was bad, it was really bad. I made a choice to work for The Man on purpose." But he wasn't happy being an "intrapreneur," and when he saw a chance to create the life of his dreams, he jumped. He believes the experience has primed his daughter for success, too, no matter what path she pursues. "Jordyn was interviewed by *Time for Kids*, which featured her on the site's home page. Since she turned nine, she has run the LEGO trivia presentation at the events. She owns it. She creates her own PowerPoint presentation. Seeing how it got started, she knows she will be able to accomplish anything she wants to. She and my son have seen it all play out. She'll succeed as long as she keeps the confidence that she has and applies it to whatever she does." Yes, she will. And so will anyone willing to take a risk and take the principles of this book to heart. Please, please, just try, if not for yourself, then for the people you love who are watching you and who want you to be happy.

You know where we are in this game? We haven't even heard the national anthem. We haven't even gotten to the parking lot. I cannot wait to see what platforms we're talking about in nine more years. I'm never afraid of the future. It's practically a national sport to reminisce about how much easier and slower life was in the past. People wonder if we're sacrificing something irreplaceable, perhaps even changing the human condition, as we become increasingly obsessed with speed and productivity. I don't worry about it because we are simply doing what we've always done, what we were probably born to do. **We wax nostalgic, but our actions betray us.** How many people above the age of thirteen in America do not have a cell phone? Practically no one. As long as we exist, humans will continue to embrace whatever inventions and innovations offer us the most speed and convenience. You're not going to lose your soul if you do this. In fact, if you're truly an entrepreneur, you're going to get it back.

ACKNOWLEDGMENTS

Five has always been my favorite number, so as I publish my fifth business book, it's especially important that I acknowledge the team that I value most in the world—my amazing wife, Lizzie; my kids, Misha and Xander; my unbelievable parents, Sasha and Tamara; and my siblings and in-laws. I am only able to live this life because of the love and the infrastructure you offer me. I thank you from the bottom of my heart.

I also want to give a huge shout-out to the entire Team GaryVee, which contributed their efforts and expertise to this book, as well as all the people that surround me on a daily basis whose talent and heart make VaynerMedia what it is. In addition, I owe enormous gratitude to the entire team at HarperBusiness, especially my editor, Hollis Heimbouch.

Finally, there is no shot that any of these books would exist without my right hand, Stephanie Land, who has collaborated with me on all five of them. She has become much more than a ghostwriter. She is my friend.

NOTES

Introduction

8   With six-figure earnings: Claire Martin, "Feel the Noise: D.I.Y. Slime Is Big Business," *New York Times*, June 25, 2017, p. 6.

8   In August 2017: Sam Gutelle, "Karina Garcia, YouTube's 'Slime Queen,' Is Heading on Tour with Fullscreen," Tubefilter.com, July 7, 2017, www .tubefilter.com/2017/07/07/karina-garcia-youtubes-slime-queen-is-heading -on-tour-with-fullscreen.

Chapter 1: The Path Is All Yours

14   YouTube's daily viewership: Feliz Solomon, "YouTube Could Be About to Overtake TV as America's Most Watched Platform," Fortune.com, Feb. 28, 2017, fortune.com/2017/02/28/youtube-1-billion-hours-television.

14   One in every five minutes: Facebook Audience Insights.

14   Every minute: Facebook Audience Insights.

14   Over 3 billion snaps: Snapchat, October 17, 2017.

14   Consequently, since 2009: "CMO Survey: Social Media Spending Falls Short of Expectations," Duke University Fuqua School of Business, news

release, Aug. 23, 2016, www.fuqua.duke.edu/news_events/news-releases/cmo-survey-august-2016/#.WPYg6I4kqV5.

14   The top-grossing YouTubers earned: Zachary Crockett, "The 10 Highest-Earning YouTube Stars Made $70.5 Million in 2016," *Vox*, Dec. 9, 2016, https://www.vox.com/culture/2016/12/9/13894186/highest-earning-youtube-stars-2016.

14   In the past, the top-grossing: Madeline Berg, "The World's Highest-Paid YouTube Stars 2015," *Forbes*, Oct. 14, 2016, https://www.forbes.com/sites/maddieberg/2015/10/14/the-worlds-highest-paid-youtube-stars-2015/#2f1cb6b53192.

14   The most popular Instagrammers: Bianca London, "How Much Are YOUR Instagram Posts Worth? Users with 1,000 Followers Could Net £4,160 a Year by Promoting Brands (and Anyone with 100,000 Can Earn More than a Lawyer), DailyMail.com, Nov. 12, 2015, www.dailymail.co.uk/femail/article-3313864/How-Instagram-posts-worth-Users-1–000-followers-net-4–160-year-promoting-brands-100–000-earn-lawyer.html.

14   The median salary: Todd Campbell, "What's the Average Income in the United States Now?" *Motley Fool*, Mar. 24, 2017, https://www.fool.com/investing/2017/03/24/whats-the-average-income-in-the-united-states.aspx.

17   "I thought . . . my voice was what I am": Peoplestaff225, "Julie Andrews: Losing My Voice Was 'Devastating,'" People.com, Mar. 20, 2015, http://people.com/movies/julie-andrews-sound-of-music-star-opens-up-about-losing-her-voice.

19   launch a new project there that aims to bridge: Natt Garun, "CNN to Start a New Media Brand with YouTube Star Casey Neistat," *Verge*, Nov. 28, 2016, www.theverge.com/2016/11/28/13762792/cnn-beme-shut-down-casey-neistat-new-startup.

Chapter 3: The Eighth Essential—Content

87   fifty extra pounds: Rich Roll, "Finding Ultra," RichRoll.com, www.richroll.com/finding-ultra.

88   the same heart disease: Camille Lamb, "Rich Roll, Vegan Ultra-Athlete,

Recovered from Alcoholism and the Standard American Diet," Miami-NewTimes.com, Oct. 27, 2012, www.miaminewtimes.com/restaurants/rich-roll-vegan-ultra-athlete-recovered-from-alcoholism-and-the-standard-american-diet-6572006.

94 His reach and popularity has spread: Adam Skolnick, "A Brutal Competition, Island to Island, in Sweden," NewYorkTimes.com, Sept. 5, 2017, https://www.nytimes.com/2017/09/05/sports/a-brutal-competition-island-to-island-in-sweden.html?_r=0.

96 In an interview with the *New York Times*: Ibid.

Chapter 5: The Only Thing You Need to Give Yourself to Crush It

122 The LEED AP exam is so rigorous: Sarah Ward, "How Hard is the LEED exam? Harder than Passing the Bar?" *Poplar*, March 14, 2014, https://www.poplarnetwork.com/news/how-hard-leed-exam-harder-passing-bar.

Chapter 8: Musical.ly

144 The company saw immediate favor: Biz Carson, "How a Failed Education Startup Turned Into Musical.ly, the Most Popular App You've Probably Never Heard Of," *Business Insider*, May 28, 2016, www.businessinsider.com/what-is-musically-2016-5/.

144 It now has 200 million users: Musical.ly Quick Stats, accessed Sept. 18, 2017.

146 As of 2012, 65 percent of new shows: Anthony Ocasio, "TV Success Rate: 65% of New Shows Will Be Canceled (& Why It Matters)," ScreenRant.com, May 17, 2012, http://screenrant.com/tv-success-rate-canceled-shows/.

Chapter 9: Snapchat

157 Despite its 173 million daily active users: Snapchat, October 17, 2017.

159 His fondness for the platform: DJ Khaled, *The Keys*, Crown Archetype, November 2016, p. 122, https://books.google.com/books?id=cpWxCwAAQBA-J&q=p+122#v=onepage&q=122&f=false.

169   women leading the way: Jenna Goudreau, "What Men and Women Are Doing on Facebook," *Forbes*, Apr. 26, 2010, https://www.forbes.com/2010/04/26 /popular-social-networking-sites-forbes-woman-time-facebook-twitter .html.

Chapter 11: YouTube

192   Increasing numbers of people: Google-commissioned Nielsen study, "You-Tube User Stats from Brandcast 2017: 3 Trends in Video Viewing Behavior," May 2017, https://www.thinkwithgoogle.com/consumer-insights/youtube -user-stats-video-viewing-behavior-trends.

Chapter 12: Facebook

209   It has almost 2 billion monthly active users: Seth Fiegerman, "Facebook Tops 1.9 Billion Monthly Users," CNN.com, May 3, 2017, http://money.cnn .com/2017/05/03/technology/facebook-earnings/index.html.

209   There are 1.15 billion daily active users: "The Top 20 Valuable Facebook Statistics—Updated November 2017," Zephoria Digital Marketing, https:// zephoria.com/top-15-valuable-facebook-statistics.

211   Mark Zuckerberg called video: Michelle Castillo, "Mark Zuckerberg Sees Video as a 'Mega Trend' and Is Gunning for YouTube," CNBC.com, Feb. 1, 2017, www.cnbc.com/2017/02/01/mark-zuckerberg-video-mega-trend-like -mobile.html.

211   In 2016, he told *BuzzFeed*: Mat Honan, "Why Facebook and Mark Zucker-berg Went All In on Live Video," *BuzzFeed News*, Apr. 6, 2016, https:// www.buzzfeed.com/mathonan/why-facebook-and-mark-zuckerberg-went -all-in-on-live-video?utm_term=.fdwpA8ZBM#.tlGzWbZG7.

211   the platform is in the process: Jon Fingas, "Facebook Will Court 'Millenni-als' with Its Original Videos," *Engadget*, May 24, 2017, https://www.engadget .com/2017/05/24/facebook-original-video-shows.

213   With 162 million views: Kurt Wagner, "'Chewbacca Mom' Was the Most Popular Facebook Live Video This Year by a Mile," *Recode*, Dec. 8, 2016,

https://www.recode.net/2016/12/8/13870670/facebook-live-chewbacca
-mom-most-popular.

213 She was rewarded handsomely: Brad Tuttle, "'Chewbacca Mom' Has Gotten $420,000 Worth of Gifts Since Facebook Video Went Viral," *Money*,
June 3, 2016, http://time.com/money/4356563/chewbacca-mom-facebook
-gifts-disney-college.

213 Hasbro, which made the original Wookie mask: Eun Kyung Kim, "'Chewbacca Mom' Now Has Her Own Action Figure Doll! Here Are the Details,"
Today, June 20, 2016, https://www.today.com/popculture/chewbacca-mom
-now-has-her-own-action-figure-doll-here-t99426.

213 She signed a multibook deal: "Zondervan Signs 'Chewbacca Mom' Candace
Payne for Multi-Book Deal," HarperCollins Christian Publishing, Jan. 17,
2017, https://www.harpercollinschristian.com/zondervan-signs-chewbacca
-mom-candace-payne-for-multi-book-deal.

213 Her first book: Candace Payne's Facebook page, accessed June 2017, https://
www.facebook.com/candaceSpayne/posts/10213133991364822.

Chapter 13: Instagram

224 In fact, on the day Stories launched: Josh Constine, "Instagram Launches
'Stories,' a Snapchatty Feature for Imperfect Sharing," *TechCrunch*, Aug. 2,
2016, https://techcrunch.com/2016/08/02/instagram-stories.

233 digital ad sales are expected: Jeanine Poggi, "Global Digital Ad Sales Will
Top TV in 2017, Magna Forecast Predicts," *Ad Age*, Dec. 5, 2016, http://adage
.com/article/agency-news/magna-digital-ad-sales-top-tv-2017/306997.

Chapter 14: Podcasts

235 as of 2014, the 139 million total commuters: Christopher Ingraham, "The
Astonishing Human Potential Wasted on Commutes," *Washington Post*
Wonkblog, Feb. 25, 2016, https://www.washingtonpost.com/news/wonk
/wp/2016/02/25/how-much-of-your-life-youre-wasting-on-your-commute
/?utm_term=.e28807a0ade3.

Chapter 15: Voice-First

246 In 2016, Google revealed: Greg Sterling, "Google Says 20 Percent of Mobile Queries Are Voice Searches," Search Engine Land, May 18, 2016, http://searchengineland.com/google-reveals-20-percent-queries-voice-queries-249917.

250 each of the eleven: planthardiness.ars.usda.gov

252 Did you know that the word *etiquette*: Richard Duffy, "Manners and Morals," introduction, Emily Post, *Etiquette: In Society, in Business, in Politics and at Home* (Funk & Wagnalls, 1922), www.bartleby.com/95/101.html.

ABOUT THE AUTHOR

GARY VAYNERCHUK is chairman and CEO of VaynerX, a $150-million-plus media holding agency that includes VaynerMedia and PureWow. He is one of the world's leading marketing experts and a four-time *New York Times* bestselling author. After growing his family wine business from a $4 million to a $60 million business, he developed and still runs VaynerMedia, one of the world's hottest digital agencies. Gary is also a prolific angel investor and venture capitalist, investing in companies including Snapchat, Facebook, Twitter, Uber, and Venmo, and cofounding the Vayner/RSE fund, among many other enterprises. He lives in New York City.